How to Steal Like an Author
Success in Writing Books Through Increased Creativity

By Dean R. Giles

Copyright Notice

© 2014 Dean R. Giles

Legal Disclaimer

Table of Contents

Contents

Robin Hood

"Every new idea is just a mashup or remix of one or more previous ideas." -- Austin Kleon

Where Did They Steal Their Ideas?

Harry Potter flashed onto existence from the mind of J.K. Rowling. She readily admits to taking ideas from local folklore. Stephanie Myers, the author of the *Twilight Series*, found the seeds of her stories in the classics, *Pride and Prejudice*, *Romeo and Juliet*, and *Wuthering Heights*. Disney based his movies on so many well-known children's stories. The seeds of creativity in authorship are found in many places. It is important to note, that ideas just don't exist in a vacuum, they are usually spawned from the seeds of earlier ideas.

I love this quote, quoted by Austin Kleon, in *Steal Like an Artist*.

Immature poets imitate, mature poets steal; bad poets deface what they take, and good poets make it into something better, or at least something different. The good poet welds his theft into a whole of feeling that is unique, utterly different from that from which it was torn.

--T.S. Eliot

So it is with writing. Capture every good idea, combine them together, add to them, take the ideas further than when you found them, then send them out into the world in a work that is unique and very much the essence of yourself, the writer.

Brandon Sanderson, author of *Mystborn*, *Elantris*, and many other books, says that he takes ideas from history and weaves them into his books.

Other writers, when asked where their ideas came from revealed the following: [1]

"They're everywhere. I'm inspired by people and things around me." Gwendolyn Brooks.

"Ideas come to a writer, a writer does not search for them." Patricia Highsmith.

"They can come from anywhere." Robert J. Conley.

Ideas for books, articles, and other writing can be found in many places and in many ways. Each person may find that the idea process is somewhat personal, that it happens for them in a way that is as unique as their writing style.

The number of ideas and the breadth of those ideas are only limited by each person's individual creativity.

Creativity, therefore, was something that intrigued me, something that enticed me to study it over a number of years. Austin Kleon's work, *Steal Like an Artist*, influenced my thinking greatly. You will see a number of quotes from his book here. Many of the concepts that he explores I had come in contact with from previous works that I have read. However, his application of the ideas is unique. He also articulates the concepts and their application very well, and he demonstrates his imagination and creativity in the actual format of his book. The format of his book is in a style completely his own.

I hope that readers of this book realize that promoting "stealing ideas" doesn't condone using them without doing something to those ideas to develop them, to make them better, and ultimately to make them unique.

Building on the Ideas of Others

Isaac Newton acknowledged the intellectual contributions of his idea predecessors in this unique and powerful way, "if I have seen further than others, it is because I was standing on the shoulders of giants."

I humbly have to acknowledge innumerable others from whom I have learned and borrowed ideas. Ideas that have ultimately come together to form this book. The back of this book has a very incomplete list of many books, articles, and resources that I have pulled ideas from. Truly, I am standing on the shoulders of giants, borrowing liberally from their ideas, and I hope that my perspective can be useful to many others out there. Take some time to browse the bibliography in the back of this book, and perhaps you will find interesting reading to add to your pool of knowledge.

Creativity

How to Increase the Creativity in Your Life

"If we're free from the burden of trying to be completely original, we can stop trying to make something out of nothing, and we can embrace influence instead of running away from it."
        –Austin Kleon

A Beautiful Mind

"Most of the things that are interesting, important, and human, are the results of creativity."
        --Mihaly Csikszentmihalyi

Figure 1 Creativity

When I first started delving into creativity, a number of the books that I read seemed to divide people into the "haves" and "have-nots." Creativity was glorified, and those that exhibited it honored and set on a pedestal. I desperately wanted to be part of that group, but I let my own insecurities whisper doubts into my ears and my mind.

I often came up with creative answers to problems and responded to miraculous inspiration, but I let myself believe that the events were flukes, just lightning flashes, that would fade and disappear. I could plainly see those creative breakthroughs that I had experienced, but I felt like they were inconsistent, and let myself believe that I really wasn't very creative.

Over a number of years, however, I found places where I could apply my creativity, and was astounded at how many ideas I had when I started to capture those ideas and put them down on paper, and how much better I was able to work through problems by relying on what I came to believe was, "out of the box" thinking.

I also realized that innovation and creativity seemed to be all around me. In looking back I am amazed at how the stories of creative people and events emphasize the flash discoveries while skimming over the years of study, preparation, hard work, failure, and disappointment that often preceded the amazing light-bulb experiences that pave the way to unbridled success.

In more recent years the tables have turned. There is a vein of study that looks at creativity from a different perspective, it has been called on occasion, generative research.

Robert Epstein, Ph.D. conducted 25 years of research. In his book, *The Big Book of Creativity Games*, he explains, "Generative research shows that novel behavior in individuals (read creativity here) is orderly and predictive, and that new ideas come from the combinations of old ideas. Creativity can be learned and fostered."

Read this again--Creativity can be learned and fostered! It can be coaxed out of most any fertile and working grey matter that exists between the ears of every person!

Among the ideas that Robert Epstein explores is the concept that everyone has pretty much the exact same creative potential, and that each of us can improve our creativity with simple exercises and games.

Through my years of study, I collected exercises meant to enhance creativity. Project management and self-development books are full of these types of exercises. In this book I want to present many of those ideas, activities, methods, and processes that have brought creative success to other people. I also want to share the lessons that I learned along the way, share some of the wisdom of others that made an impression on me, and share my enthusiasm for opening up your world to the creative potential inside of you that is yearning to get out.

In the final section of this book, I attempt to apply creative exercises directly to writing. There isn't a field in this world that requires more creativity, innovation, and persistence than the field of writing. Your success as a writer will depend on how well you can creatively combine and develop ideas and concepts that are specific to the themes and subjects of your books and articles.

The up-side of this situation is that writers often have better creative habits than other people, they tend to grasp the concepts easily, see their greater application, and they usually find immediate improvement in their writing when they integrate just a few of the many creativity activities into their current methods and processes. This book is for everyone wanting more creativity in their lives, but it has been carefully tailored to specifically help authors and writers.

Creativity Starts from the Inside

One of the quotes from Star Wars that I hear referred to often is from Yoda, "Do or do not, there is no try."

Creativity is an action, it comes from inside. It won't be perfect, and there will ever be something more you can do to it. But, it is an action pure and simple. Just do it. Don't try to put it off, don't defer it to someone else, just get out of your comfort zone and do it.

A fable or object story that I heard from my father went something like this. Two frogs fell into a bucket of cream. The other frogs gathered around and watched. The two frogs swam, and kicked, and tried desperately to get out. As some time went on, the other frogs began to mock their efforts. "You'll never get out. You just aren't strong enough. There's just no way you will get out of this mess." One of the frogs heard the spectators, and finally just gave up and sank to the bottom of the bucket. The other frog, however, was a little deaf. He could hear the commotion up above, but couldn't understand a word that was being said. He figured that the other frogs were shouting encouragement to him, so he worked all the harder. Over some time, the cream began to turn to butter. The frog was able to get up on a little bit of solidity, and finally jump out.

Every adventure into creativity will be accompanied by a cacophony of voices. The voices will be all around you. Some will be encouraging voices, others will be full of criticism, and some filled with envy. Choose carefully the voices that you listen to, but realize, that the voice that makes the most difference is the one that comes from inside of you. When that voice has clarity, it will quiet all of the outside voices, and will lead you to the creative successes you desire.

Understand and never doubt that you are creative! Remind yourself that you are creative often, it reaffirms that truth again and again. Often the only real difference between a creative person and a not-so-creative person is their own beliefs. Any person, that believes he or she is creative, can tap into that part of their mind that contains solutions that are only available through creativity.

Creative people can find ways to:

Generate ideas at will
Find new ways to make things work
Know where to look for the best ideas.
Create new book ideas
Improve old book ideas to create new ones.
Develop powerful solutions to current problems
See problems as new opportunities.
Be the idea person that other people come to.
Manipulate and modify ideas until they come up with the most innovative and powerful ones to work with.

In the next chapter I discuss the foundation of creativity.

"You're Never Gonna Slow Me Down"

How to Remove Roadblocks to Creativity

Doubt, fear, and confusion are the antithesis to creativity. You must work to counter your own fears. Here is an activity that is a good way to remove fear and doubt, I call it "Counter Point."

Crush Fear and Doubt with this counterpoint activity.

Write down every fear or doubt. Then write a counterpoint to it that answers every fear or issue.

For example:

Fear
I might as well not bring up my ideas, no one really listens to me any way.

Counter Point
I have great ideas. My ideas often make a difference. People will listen to me, and like my ideas.

Fear
This idea is so different that I'll be laughed at if I suggest it.

Counter Point
Even if others reject my idea, they will respect those who try to show creativity and innovation. Others will see that I am trying to improve the situation. Sometimes the riskier the idea, the greater the reward when it works.

Fear
I'll never be able to do it.

Counter Point
I'll take it a little bit at a time. I'll set up a schedule to do a little bit every day. When I see how much I have accomplished, I will be amazed.

Any time a doubt or fear raises up its ugly head, smash it flat with a counter point. You will be surprised at how quickly you will squelch those fears, and let your creativeness loose on your projects and problems.

Assertions and Affirmations

Exercises for increasing creativity

I have read a number of books that promote one process or another for success in creativity. Most of these books have their own step-by-step process that leads someone to "creative" thinking. After trying many of them, and after watching how creativity works with me and with my teams, I now believe that creative processes are not linear. I believe that they have a tendency to bounce around and to take you on detours that zig-zag you from one activity to another.

To illustrate what I mean, my family and I have hiked many mountain paths. The paths that go straight up the mountain are exhausting, they are steep and very difficult to travel. When it rains, the water runs right down the path, usually digging out gullies and ridges that become obstacles in the path for future hikers.

This last year we were at Zion's National Park, we hiked a path that lead to a destination called Angel's Landing. One section of that path is a manmade section that is reinforced with brick and mortar. It is called "Walter's Wiggles," and it zig-zags back and forth 24 times from the bottom to the top of the hill-face that we scale at that point. While on that path, every corner seemed like a detour, it felt like such a burden sometimes to flow from one side to the other, but when you see it from a distance, you realized that each level is essential, and that each corner brings you closer to your goal.

I'm going to point out some "touch-stones," some corners, that have marked the path to creativity that I have witnessed in the past. You may not need each one of these, but each one may come in handy, so I will mention them here.

Creativity Challenge – Believe In Yourself

One of the theories about creativity that I find again and again, is the principle that creative people don't just believe that they are creative, they **KNOW** that they are creative. They have convinced themselves that they are creative. Often this starts with very simple seeds. Take out a piece of paper. Write down a simple affirmation that you are creative. Now write it 15 to 20 different ways. Make sure that you use the first person, second person, and third person perspectives in your sentences. They would look something like this:

I am a creative person. Dean, you are a creative person. Dean is a very creative person. I bring creativity to every activity. Dean is always creative in his solutions...

Keep going and put down 15 to 20 sentences like the ones above. Now do this every day for three weeks. If, after three weeks, you still have doubts, do it for another three weeks.

Anytime you find yourself doubting your ability or creativity, start another three week cycle. Creativity will change your life and become a part of what and who you are. If you go forward with this challenge, you will come to know that you are creative and can handle any creative challenge.

Who Wants to be a Millionaire?

How to Jumpstart Creativity with Questions

Who wants to be a Millionaire is a classic television game show. Contestants get 12 questions that they have to answer. They are rewarded with some cash for every question that they answer correctly, losing all of the previously won cash if they answer incorrectly. If they answer all 12 questions correctly, they take home one million dollars. Answering the questions correctly can make a contestant very rich.

In writing and in creativity answering the right questions can make you successful. But, ASKING the right questions can make your book or project phenomenal!

If there were a single principle of creativity that would give you the most value or bang for the effort, it would be the principle of asking the right questions. Often the problem or challenge that you face is just the tip of the iceberg. It is the portion that you see.

Figure 2 Iceberg

When you start to think about your problem or challenge, and begin to look at it through different perspectives, you might see much more than you realized on the surface. Creativity starts with asking the right questions. Often the answers that you get depends on the question that you ask. Creative solutions flow effortlessly when asking the right questions.

An example of this was taught to me through another story that my father told to me. He and his friends visited a local malt shop when they were younger, and the owner of the shop also made the malts. He sold a few other grocery items in the shop as well, and as Christmas rolled around, he found that he could sell a little Egg Nog for the holidays. He found he had to order more eggs to keep up with the demand. After the holidays, he forgot to cut down the number of eggs that he ordered, and found himself in a dilemma, specifically more eggs than he could sell. He thought about adding an egg to his malts, and charging a little bit more for the malt with the egg. The experiment didn't go so well at first, as he asked his customers if they would like an egg in their malt. However, he began to see a lot of success when he changed the question. He asked each customer if they wanted one or two eggs in their malt. Suddenly his sales of eggs in malts increased dramatically.

The next exercise for increasing creativity is to first start with rephrasing the question.

Rephrase the question

People who are credited with very creative ideas often have LOTS of ideas. It is estimated that only about 30% of Beethoven's, Mozart's, and other famous musical composers' works are currently played. The other 70% isn't well known and not performed at all. The brilliant pieces that we know and love are a relatively small portion of the total body of works by these famous creative people. Part of their success was simply producing a large volume of works.

Producing a lot of ideas is a foundational principle.
Produce lots and lots of ideas. Learn to train your intuition to help you choose later which ideas to pursue, but put out the ideas every day. I want to also suggest that when you are in idea production mode, that you turn off most of the internal sensors. Don't judge the ideas at this point, or censure them. That can come later.

The first exercise of asking the right question is to rephrase the question. The exercise is simple:
On a clean piece of paper, or at the top of a new file, write the question or problem in the most explicit way you can think of. Then quickly rephrase the question a number of times looking for different ways of stating it and different ways to get to the same or similar results.

For example, if my problem was that I needed to sell more books to make more money, I might start with a sentence like this:

How do I sell more books to create more income from my book business?

Then I would list the other ways of rephrasing my problem.

How can I get my book in front of more people so that they will buy more copies?
How do I find more customers for my books?
How do I write more books, so that more books are sold?
How do I advertise to the kinds of people that will buy my books?
How do I make more money from each book?
How do I make my book more enticing to more people?
How do I get partners to help me sell my books?
Where can I promote my books to prepared buyers?
What else can I do with my books to get more people to buy them?
How do I get more reviews, so more people will consider buying my book?

Are there questions that these questions suggest?

It is interesting to look at what you came up with off the top of your head, then look just a little further for avenues of thought that you hadn't considered before.

In the example above, there are numerous aspects of selling more books that were never even mentioned in the original problem. Now it is easy to see that among those forgotten aspects are customers, writing more books, advertising, partners, reviews, and price. Each of these aspects could be pursued for possible solutions or additional avenues for expanding my efforts.

The Originals

How to Get to Original Ideas

The trick is being able to look at the same information everyone else sees, but organize it in a way that is new and different. You need to see a new pattern that is being over-looked by the masses. New patterns are what will create new and original ideas.

I use these tools to organize the data differently:

Fishbone Diagram

What are the possible causes of the problem or question? Can you chart them out in a fishbone diagram? The fishbone diagram starts with a head that summarizes the problem. Then a straight line that is the conduit to the problem. Each of the causes are graphed out at 45 degree angles.

Here is the fishbone diagram for the "sell more books" problem.

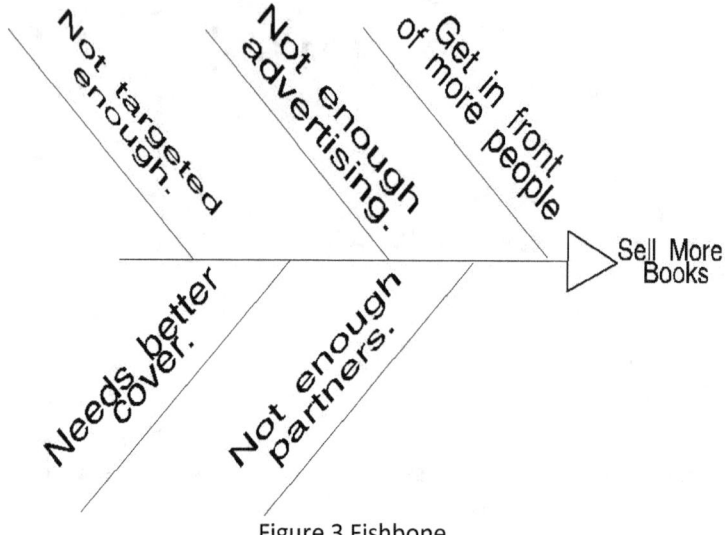

Figure 3 Fishbone

Mind Map

Use a mind map to plot out questions and sub-questions that can really help you organize your thoughts, see patterns, and get what you want to talk about organized. You can find free mind map software from Xmind or FreeMind, or you can use a large sheet of butcher or poster paper.

Start with your central idea in the middle of the page. As you think of ideas related to your central idea, connect those ideas with lines. The sub ideas are connected to the major ideas and so on.

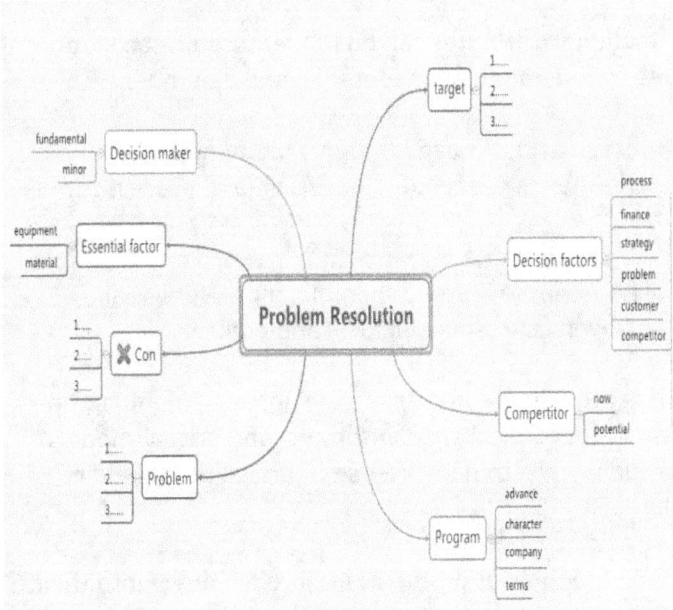

Figure 4 Mind Map

Slice and Dice

Every problem or challenge has a set of attributes. Those include the materials they are made of, the way things are gathered, how they are distributed, methods of construction, methods of finance, advertising, support, partners, and the list could go on.

There are ways to define those attributes:

Descriptive, functional, by process, socially, and by price.

Descriptive attributes can include color, size, shape, structure, material, texture, density, space, sound, and taste.

Functional attributes can be full-featured, specialized, integrated, modular, disposable, and dependent.

Process attributes can be supply, manufacturing, distribution, sales models, licensing, and processes over time.

Social attributes can be sharable, digital/physical, controversial, responsibilities, and politics.

Price attributes can be price to suppliers, manufacturers, wholesalers, retailers, consumers, and pricing models including free to paid, licensed, time-allotted, and multi-tiered.

Once products or problems are broken down into their respective attributes then the different options for attributes can be listed. Each option can be considered individually, or a cross-section of options considered for complete packages.

For Your Eyes Only

How to Look at Your Problem or Challenge

A Rhinoceros has a hard time seeing what is directly in front of him, people can sometimes suffer from the same ailment.

The human mind tries relentlessly to simplify and reduce. Things like driving and playing the piano become more and more routine, the complex judgments that were needed to start these activities or do them for the first time get reduced. Soon, you don't even have to think much while you do them.

The same thing happens with our observation. As we become acquainted with an area, a path, or a place, we no longer notice many details about that place.

Creative people turn that around. They learn to observe and see what other people miss and pass right on by. Learning how to be observant takes some work, but is worth the effort. Here are some activities that can help:

We all live in the Yellow Submarine

For a day, notice everything that is yellow. Watch during your daily travels, observe in your work area, look over the neighborhood. What things do you see that are yellow.

A few days later, change the color to blue. Now note everything that is blue through the day.

Did you see anything new during your observations? Did it surprise you how many things you had missed in the past—even if you had made those same trips many times, and worked in that same office for some years.

Van Gogh had a time where he seemed fixated on the color yellow.

Many creative solutions come from observation. The observation of how burs cling to clothing and animal fur was the basis for the invention of Velcro.

Another exercise could be the following:

On a different day, stop on your way to work or to the grocery store. Notice your surroundings. How does one house or yard differ from another? What is unusual about this spot?

When you discover how things are different, you can make remote connections that explain the differences, or show how they are still the same. That is the type of daily practice that will help make you more creative day after day.

Be the Ball

In Disney's animated movie, Ants, the ants form together to make a wrecking ball. One of the ants gives these words of advice, "be the ball." It is good advice for creative people. When looking at a problem or possible solution, change your perspective. What would it be like to be the document in the process? Where does the document go? What happens to it on its trip to being processed? Looking from the viewpoint of a specific object, or a specific user in the system can produce creative solutions from brand new perspectives.

To Infinity and Beyond

"It is easier to enhance creativity by changing conditions in the environment than by trying to make people think more creatively."
          --Mihaly Csikszentmihalyi

Figure 5 Environment

What is your environment like at work, in your study, or where you go to write? For the most creativity, you need to surround yourself with thought enhancing objects. Pixar understands this concept very well. Walk into their studio and you will see large statues and objects from their movies. People's work areas can be physical mockups of their movie houses or movie themes.

Make your work environment more exciting. Try some of the following:

Put art work on your walls. Find prints with lots of detail, that you can stop and explore from time to time.

On the other end of the spectrum is the idea of putting up art or prints that depict your idea of peace, and tranquility. Taking a break from the chaos can clear your mind and improve its effectiveness.

Keep clay, Legos, and other building materials close at hand. Build something, doodle, or just roll something around in your hands when you are bored, or transitioning from one activity to the next. Your hands see the world in a unique way, and are always seeking a way to express those views.

Print pictures of your goals or vision and put them on the walls or your desk. A goal unwritten is only a wish. You can make those wishes and dreams more concrete by creating and printing out images that depict what you are working towards.

Lessons Learned

How to Learn About Your Subject

"Don't wait until you know who you are before you get started."
>--Austin Kleon

"A genuinely creative accomplishment is almost never the result of a sudden insight, a lightbulb flashing on in the dark, but comes after years of hard work."
>--Mihaly Csikszenmihalyi

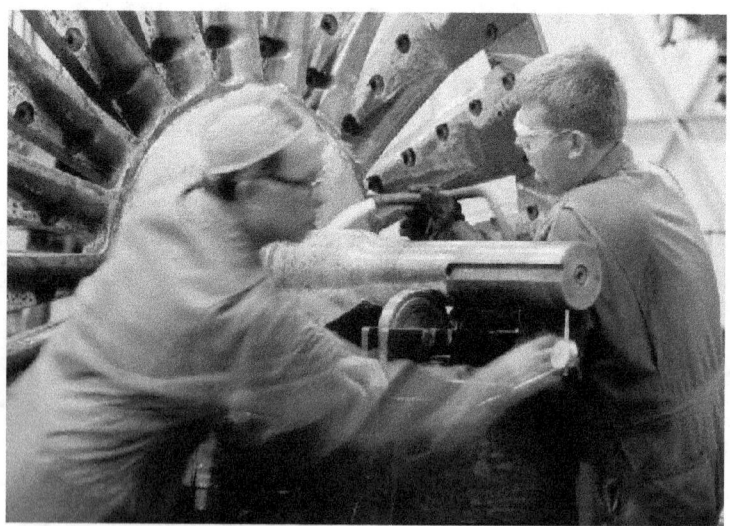

Figure 6 Hard Work

Have you ever heard the expression, "the blind leading the blind?" A key to being an effective teacher is to do some studying first. Dig deep into your domain. Understand the whys behind the principles. Explain them in your own words and develop your own examples. When you write or talk about a subject, you will have enough knowledge to "lead" people to where they need to go.

Most of your best ideas are going to come from remote connections, from pasting together separate ideas that when combined give you more than the sum of the two separately. Keep in mind that great new ideas come from a mashup of old ideas turned to solve a new problem.

With that background, you can understand that being deep in your areas of expertise is important, but being broad in a whole lot of other areas is next most important thing.

Learn a lot about many things. Watch the discovery channel. Pick up magazines and scan the articles. Read about or watch the news. Understand what is popular and important in the public consciousness. All of these things will give you a broader base to pull from.

Here are some exercises that can enhance the broadness of your education:

Read new magazines: Take advantage of trips to the doctor's office, dentist, or hair stylist by picking up magazines that are different than anything you would normally read. Browse the articles and the advertisements. What themes seem to come up repeatedly? What questions are asked in the headlines? What pops off of the page for you in particular? Can you figure out why it pops off of the page?

Search the Internet. During the day, did you hear something that caught your attention? Did you learn a new word, or hear of a new place. Go ahead and take ten or fifteen minutes to dig into it. What did the word mean? Can you use it in a sentence now? Where is the new place? Could you tell someone else a little about that new place now that you have looked it up? Don't forget to look at images about the place, word, or new concept that you decided to look up. Images can make learning faster and give the learning more longevity in your consciousness.

Read do-it-yourself manuals, and watch how-to programs. Watching television programs, or YouTube clips that show you how to do things, or how things are made can equip you with lots of ideas of how to make your ideas work and give them reality. Reading how-to books teaches you the art of instructions. Not just how to follow them, but how to write about them.

Learn about different places by traveling. Take the opportunity to take a trip. Visit local historical sights, go out of the country when you get a chance. So much of what we know and understand comes from a culture that we grow up in and learn to operate within. Notice what is different when you travel to different places.

When I visited Mexico, I was enchanted with the little shops and outdoor markets. I found that everyone was a "negociante," a business person, and that on top of their job, they might make, grow, or simply sell something out in the markets. I found that for most people, making ends meet financially was difficult, and that the traveling markets, and outdoor shops were just the requirements of the culture to survive. I discovered that even children knew how to subtly dicker on prices, how to catch your attention, and keep it for as long as possible, while displaying their wares.

The Accidental Tourist

When you go somewhere new, be a tourist. Sample the new experiences. Take a walk around the block. Explore the airport, bus station, or other places that you might be for the first time. I found the airport, the city information kiosks, and bus terminals to be places of interest. See what you might find at these places that you won't find anywhere else. Why are those things found at the airport or the bus station?

Read, Read, Read

Reading avidly will help your skills as a writer. Stephen King's advice to writers, is read, read, read. While visiting the school that one of my children attended, I saw a poster. The poster was the picture of a boy and a girl composed completely of fruits and vegetables. The caption was, "You are what you eat." It is also very true that you are what you read and ingest intellectually. Feed you mind with new experiences and new knowledge.

Be a Collector

There is a difference between a collector and a hoarder. The collector finds things of value, organizes them, and often displays them in the best light and setting. A hoarder simply amasses objects regardless of their value, and often hides them away without any organization or display. Be a collector and not a hoarder.

Organize Your Collections

Find a note book, open a file on your computer, pull out a 3X5 card, or pack around a deck of sticky notes. Use these things to take notes on your travels, jot down all of your ideas and the connections that you see between ideas, and between those ideas and their applications. You will be amazed at how quickly you can fill up a notebook. Try to create categories and try to organize your thoughts and ideas.

If you can find the notes that you took on certain subjects or ideas at a later time, you can expand on those notes. I often jot things down in a journal or a notebook, then organize the thoughts and ideas later. The organization helps me to remember the ideas, but it also lets me have a little bit of incubation time with those thoughts. I will sometimes have other ideas to add to the ones that I wrote down originally, just because I had some time to think about them and digest them.

Let's Get Physical

How to Make it Real

"In my experience, it's in the act of making things and doing our work that we figure out who we are."
--Austin Kleon

Figure 7 Making

You have often heard that a picture is worth a 1000 words. Don't discount the value of doodles, quick drawings, pictures, images, or objects made from clay or other building material. A model can often portray more than any number of explained ideas. If something can be better explained with a quick picture—go ahead and create the drawing, take the photo, or collect the image.

I recently learned of an amazing new invention is called the 3D printer. This device repeatedly lays down layers of polymer plastic. The layers build on each other as instructed by a program in the printer and some specific input by a user. The object is built one miniscule layer at a time. When the printer is done, a three dimensional object is complete. It is the object designed on the computer screen. The output from the printer is a real three dimensional plastic object.

What that means is that the exact size and shape of an object that someone wants to build out of other materials can be created out of plastic with this printer to see how the object will actually look and feel and how it will work in the space that it has been designed for.

Prototypes can be made easily and inexpensively with the printer, shortening the development cycle for these types of physical goods, and making them less expensive to develop as well.

Think about ways to model your ideas. How could you produce simple models or substitutes that could be used as proof of concept? If you had a model of the object in your hands, what else could you do with it? Perhaps you could mimic the uses that the real object will be employed in doing, just to see how it might perform or be perceived.

The Life of PI

Figure 8 Journal

Do you keep a journal? Keeping a journal may help your creative side by getting you used to giving voice to your feelings and thoughts. Finally, be sure to keep an idea log. Keep a journal of just your ideas and how those ideas develop as you think about them and as you do something about those ideas.

Much of what we know about the lives of creative people of the past come from their journals and their idea logs. Going back over a week, a month, or even a year of your creative ideas can create an amazing boost to your current creativity.

Hero Quest

How to Discover Your Idea Genealogy

"Climb your own family tree." -- Austin Kleon

Who are your heroes? Who has influenced what you think, who you are, and what you have become? Do you have any authors or creators that you admire? Make a list of your heroes, then read about them. Go to the bibliographies of the books that you read about those heroes, and see if any of the books referenced in the bibliography are available at the library. Read the things that have influenced your heroes, and understand them at a deeper level. This kind of learning will enhance your depth, your broadness of learning, and your understanding of the things and people that you love and admire. Find attributes that you like from your heroes and try to imitate those attributes.

Alice in Wonderland

Have you ever listened to children make-believe? In an instant they can be in a whole new world. They can be princes and princesses, spies or adventurers. A hill in the back yard can be the world's largest mountain, and a simple stick, a magic scepter.

That kind of imagination can drive creativity in very practical ways. Take time out to play. To imagine the world as it should be or as it could be. Devise wild explanations for why things are the way that you imagined them in your imagined world, or to explain away how things got to where you imagined they should or could be.

What could have happened to bring them to that imagined end or utopia? Perhaps you can't bring the utopia about that you imagined, but are there things that could be done in the here and now that could bring your world closer to that imagined world that is so desirable.

Make your goals more tangible by imagining the world as it would be after you have accomplished your goal. If you can believe in this world, it can be made a reality.

Back to the Future

There is another principle of creativity that goes hand in hand with imagining your goals. It starts with imagining your desired goal, or your problem being solved, or the best case scenario that you wanted to happen coming about. Now work your way back logically from there. What possibly could have happened to cause that ultimate goal to have come to reality? Did you get the raise you imagined? Did you acquire several new, high end customers? Did your investments pay off in unforeseen ways?

Now take one step further back. What caused you to get that raise, did you get an industry certification? Did you take a course at the local business college? Or what caused you to get the new clients? Did you offer a new service? Did you enhance the service you now offer? Did you enter into a partnership to build out your portfolio? What happened with your investment? Did you diversify? Did you find better places to put your money? Did you hire a new investment manager?

Do you see how this works? Start from the end—the very far future, where the world has come together to create exactly the outcome that you desired. Now what could have possibly caused that end result to happen? Make a list. Write down all of the possibilities you can come up with. Come up with the most incredible explanations for why this happened, and all of the most plausible ones. Then work your way back to today. What needed to happen to cause your possibilities?

Finally, make it real. What can you do today that would start the world down one of those paths of possibilities? Once you know the end, and can truly believe it, then you can begin to build that end by working back from the future—your future, the way that you see it and desire it.

Do You See What I See?

In the Lego Movie, the master builders could automatically see the Lego pieces that would be required for every project. I used to be an appliance repairman. I have looked at hundreds of schematics and technical drawings. What fascinates me with those types of drawings is how it all fits together. The details of how a motor fits to a pulley and the pulley to a belt, and the belt to a rotor, and so on to make something that will wash your clothes or something that will mix ingredients together to make bread.

When you are imagining the world that you want, go ahead and look a little deeper. If you imagined a world where you would never need to shovel snow from your sidewalk, perhaps you could imagine a matrix of small wires underneath the surface of the sidewalk that would keep the sidewalk warm enough to melt the snow, or perhaps you could imagine an automated tarp that extends when it snows or rains to protect your sidewalk. Whatever your goal might be, when you imagine it, look a little deeper? What do you see? What could you use to build it? What would the insides look like?

During those moments when you are doodling, or when you have some clay, Legos, or tinker toys, model what the insides would look like. Sketch out how things might go together. The creative process that lets you "play" with the construction of your ideas, can also let you see better ways to build and put things together. It can draw out ideas that are tied to the means and materials of creation. You begin to understand your world and goals better than you ever did before.

A River Runs Through it

I love a walk down the river trail not far from our house. The sights and smells of the river and the leisurely pace that I take when I walk it are relaxing and refreshing. Learning to relax and let all of the tension and worries of the day dissipate is another principle of creativity. A spring that is always tight will quickly loose its tension and ability to do what it was made for. Your mind and spirit are no different they require times to relax and let your mind wander.

Take time every day to unwind and forget the problems and issues of the day. Take an evening every week to take a night out with your wife or significant other, and just enjoy the company. Take a day a month to schedule recreation, and take a week a year for a vacation.

The amazing thing about your mind is that it continues to make subconscious connections to your problem in the background, but it needs a time when you aren't focusing on anything in particular. Taking time out for play, relaxation, and refreshment are as important as focusing when you are working and being productive.

The tranquility of a river and the idea of trying to create a relaxing atmosphere was incorporated into Salt Lake City's City Creek Mall. The city creek really does run through the mall. The creek has fish, waterfalls, and there is a pool with fountains, music, and fire that is used to put on a show every hour or so.

Just be sure to take time to relax and let your mind move away from the problems of the day. Your mind will continue to work on your problems in the background, and you will often see remote connections to what you are working on during those times that you are really relaxed and thinking about other things.

Multiplicity

"Manipulation is the brother of creativity...Remember that everything new is just an addition or modification to something that already existed."
    --Michael Michalko

Great ideas are born from modifying what you are currently doing or modifying the current solutions. There is an acronym for the multiple methods that you can use. The acronym is SCAMPER. Below are modification methods which fill out the letters to the acronym.

Substitute

What can be substituted? What can be exchanged? What else could it be used instead? Look at the building materials, the services, the distribution methods, and the products themselves.

In 1901 King Camp Gillette created disposable blades for a very different razor. He ushered in the era of disposable razors by substituting a small, replaceable blade for the long barber's blade that everyone was using. It was a huge success.

Adapt

"Make it a habit to keep on the lookout for novel and interesting ideas that others have used successfully. Your idea needs to be original only in its adaptation to the problem you are working on"
    --Thomas Edison
People are constantly adapting to their circumstances. Can you adapt your ideas, your products, and your books to your own unique circumstances?

Arthur Fry had a glue that wouldn't cure. It didn't hold things securely enough, but he took that glue that remained tacky, and created the sticky note with it. Today, that adaptation is used by the millions in offices and homes around the United States.

Look at your problem or challenge and ask, what else is like this? Are there any situations that you have experienced that offer a parallel? What successful product could you copy? What other context could you put this in? If it is working well for tax accountants, could it be modified to work for bankers, or maybe retailers?

Can you alter the physical characteristics to make it different or better? Make it smaller, or much larger, make it more environmentally friendly, or more convenient? What bothers you the most about other similar solutions? Could you fix what is wrong, or what makes it cost the most?

Little adaptations can change an entire product, or other adaptations can make the product just right for your solution.

Combine

Most new ideas are a combination of old ideas. Look for remote connections where ideas can be connected at the intersections. Welding those ideas together is the principle of combining.

For example:

At the intersection of a laptop and a telephone is the smart-phone which brings some of the features of both to a single device. Apple, Blackberry, and dozens of other Android look-a-likes are riding that combination to great profits.

The Pillow Pet is a combination of a plush stuffed animal and a pillow for children. When the pillow is folded up, it is a play toy for the child, when it is unlatched, it can be used as a pillow.

Finding remote connections and forcing combinations is a recipe for amazing creativity. This book is a result of combining creativity and authorship. The skills of discovering remote connections can be learned and practiced.

Activity for Learning and Practicing Remote Connections

On your way to work or in your travels. Observe what is around you. What objects do you see that you can form a connection about to your problem or challenge? What do you see people doing that could be applied to your problem or challenge?

As an example, I had a programming challenge that had me trying to create several classes to handle different data types. Each new type added a new level of complexity to the problem and gave me one more code path to worry about. On the train ride to work, the train passes through a few rural areas. I noticed the sprinkler lines that connect together and have wheels to help position them in the field. I noticed that the end pipe had a large cap that could be removed to clean out the pipe. I realized that my problem was much like the pipe with water in it. The data was the water, and there were different sprinklers where the water would come out. I realized that I could create just one data path, and separate the data just at the very end. If I ran into a data type that I hadn't planned for, I could let it fall out of the end—like the clean-out at the end of the pipe, then handle it there. This changed my program completely, and simplified it immensely. The idea came to me as a remote connections activity.

Modify

As an appliance repairman, I had a cable that could extend power to a stove, but I was going to need to create a second one for dryers, then I would have to carry both around when I traveled. I really didn't like that solution. I found that I could modify the receptacle so that it could accommodate both the stove and the dryer plugs. A simple modification was able to reduce my tool box to just packing one cable that did the job of two things.

What can you modify about your idea that would extend its use or make it practical for other things? When Apollo 13 had an unexpected air leak, the engineers on earth had to take a set of similar materials as those found on the space craft, modify them, and create a solution to the problem. There is an art to modification. Look for ways to modify what you make and what you write to fit other circumstances.

Minimize

Where are the biggest problems?

Can you minimize the problems, cut costs, make objects smaller, or make them less visible? If you can't eliminate something, can you minimize it or minimize its effect?

The telephone has been minimized again and again until it fits into your pocket. Google has mimicked the old Dick Tracy wrist watch phone, and now has a phone and a search device that sits on your wrist—in the "smart watch."

Put to Other Uses

Can you retarget the use of your products or ideas? Find a new use for an old item, or look for ways to use something for its side effect.

In the software business, we have a concept we call "verticals." What is meant by verticals is that the software that is developed is likely to be used as a general purpose software. However, with a few tweaks, it could be developed specifically for doctor's offices. That would be one vertical. If it were changed a little it could be specific for lawyer's offices, then that would be a second vertical. The idea is to take something that is suited to a general purpose, then modify it to be very specific. Then modify it again to be very specific for something else.

Changing the demographics is another way to put to other uses. Could your product be made to appeal to teens? What about seniors? To Boomers, or to Millennials?

What about industries? Could your product be specialized for home building?

What about for manufacturing? What about for retail?...

Exercise for putting things to other uses:

Break down your product, service, or non-fiction book into its key attributes.

Make a list of the attributes.

Now make a list for each attribute that would suggest a new audience or a specific group of people that it could be used differently for or adapted for.

Eliminate

Have you ever used a disposable razor or a paper plate? These items were designed by taking away the expensive materials that made them durable. This eliminated the biggest costs of the items and allowed them to be used then discarded.

Calculator companies make the internal chips for their high end calculators and the low-end calculators exactly the same, but they disable and eliminate specific functions on the low-end products.

The tablet computer eliminates many things from laptops that make them thinner, lighter, and more mobile.

Take something that is very successful as it is and look for ways to eliminate features or functions. The more compact, lighter, and more specialized an item becomes, the better it will solve specific problems, and it has the potential to be even more successful and popular than the full featured item.

Replace

One of my favorite tools, while camping, is my combination spoon, fork, and knife. It is kind of like a Swiss Army Knife, but it only has three blades. The idea is that I unfold the utensil that I want to use. When I get done with that utensil, I wash it and fold it back up. I replace that utensil blade with a different one, if needed, for the next meal. The tool becomes a spoon, or a fork, or a knife, depending upon which blade I pull out.

Another example is my electric drill. It can become an electric screwdriver if I just replace the drill bit with a screwdriver head. Or my drill becomes a power buffer when I replace the drill bit with a buffing head. I can use it to polish my car or furniture.

When you come up with new ideas. How can you make them more versatile by replacing one part with another? Could you make them serve many purposes by creating a portion that is replaceable?

Look for ways to create new things by replacing something in the old one.

Remember the acronym SCAMPER and apply the above concepts to improve creativity in your ideas and solutions.

Toppling the Tower

A tower can be a difficult thing to climb or scale, but take the same tower, lay it on its side, and it becomes accessible to everyone.

This exercise has helped me topple some of the biggest towers that I have run into:

Write down all of the reasons that you are sure something just won't work.

Then one at a time reverse the assumptions.

Here is an example:

I won't get hired because I don't have a degree.
I won't get the raise because I don't have experience with the new tools.
I can't get out of this dead-end job because my company doesn't have any openings higher up the chain.

Often there are a number of things that we just "know" are stopping our progress or not letting us get what we want or need. If we reverse those assumptions— pretending that they have already been solved, occasionally, we can see how to get around that road block.

Here are what the sentences look like if we reverse the assumptions.

I got hired without a degree because I started taking classes online.
I got the raise because I started learning the new tools, and impressed the boss with my ambition.

I got out of the dead-end job by cross-training and changing departments.

Look at the end result. Pretend that the end result IS the new reality. In your mind the end result has already happened. Now just explain how that desired end result came to be, and explain how it happened. Take the reason or excuse that you used in the past and reverse it to find out what has been stopping you, and how you can get around the impediment. See the problem without the assumptions and brand new opportunities begin to appear.

Just Around the River Bend

In Disney's film, Pocahontas, the chief tells Pocahontas that she should be as steady as the river, but she sees it completely differently, that the river is always changing and presents new opportunities at every bend.

Figure 8 River Bend

My grandmother often said, "Life is what happens while you are planning other things." Turn the disappointments and surprises into opportunities. I was laid off, and when I found the next job, it included a commute that I wasn't fond of. However, I was able to change my habits and began to ride the train. Riding the train actually increased my commute time, but I was able to write on the train.

What setbacks have you experienced in your life? What lessons have you learned from those setbacks? What skills have you acquired while zig-zagging back and forth at unscheduled and unplanned-for stops along the way? How can you use those new, and unexpected "opportunities" to your advantage?

Choose the Right

If you are using the exercises and principles that have been presented this far, you are beginning to acquire a lot of new ideas. You might be getting files and notebooks full of them. How do you choose which ones to pursue?

Best Bang for the Buck

Look at your projects from a value perspective. Which project will bring you the most money? Which one will cost the least to implement? What are the costs of starting, or the costs of doing a proof of concept? Which projects do you have the most enthusiasm for? If you are excited about a project, you may stick with it longer, and have a better chance of seeing it completed quickly. Where can you see the most success the fastest? Both money and success like speed. Sometimes it pays to pick the project that you can complete the fastest. Success breeds success. Once you have a successful project under your belt, then you have an even better chance of completing a second one. The experience that you gain will grow into a sort of intuition. You will start to see the projects that have the best possibilities of being successful, and the ones that don't.

Choosing the right projects to work on is an art. You need to work on it often and persistently.

All of the creativity exercises and ideas can be applied directly to writing books. I present how to apply them in the second part of this book.

CREATING BOOKS

How to Steal Like an Author

"An idea or product that deserves the label "creative" arises from the synergy of many sources not just from the mind of one person."
    --Mihaly Czikszentmihalyi,

We have all heard that good ideas don't exist in a vacuum, but do we truly believe it? Austin Kleon, in his recent book, *Steal Like An Artist*, explores the concept that creativity comes from "stealing" from the masters. I really enjoyed his book, and admit that I stole from his ideas.

I hope to show you throughout this book that good and successful ideas and models did not suddenly appear over-night, that they had their origins much earlier as someone else's ideas. New ideas are mostly adaptations of the old ideas with new applications to present problems.

Here is a screen full of books that revolve around the ideal of "stealing". It is an old concept and is still very popular. I used the Amazon search bar to get the following results:

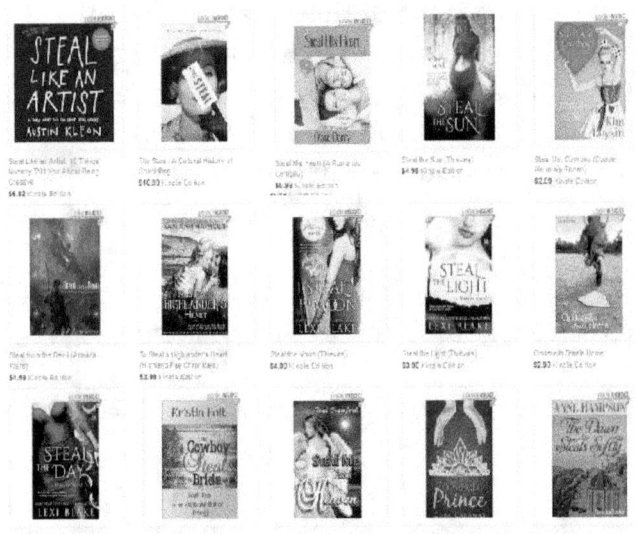

Figure 9 Steal

"It's not where you take things from—It's where you take them to" --Jean-Luc Godard.

I love a sketch in Calvin and Hobbs, a cartoon strip that shows Calvin just discovering the implications of "evolution." He tell Hobbs, his stuffed tiger and imaginary friend, "Wow, millions of years have culminated to produce me!"

Hobbs replies, "So what are you going to do?" The next scene shows the two of them watching cartoons together.

Discovering good ideas is very important, but much more important than that is the soul-searching question: What are you going to do with the ideas? Where will you take them? Will you stand on the shoulders of the giants who got you here to produce something that extends their work and propagates their ideas further into the future?

Pablo Picasso understood the concept.

"Good artists copy, great artists steal." –Pablo Picasso

If you steal the idea, and it becomes yours, you take ownership of it, and can change and develop it at will. It has been said, if you steal from one person, that is plagiarism, but, if you steal from 100 people, now that's research. Take liberally from many sources. Let the ideas mix and marinate together, then see how your mind can sort them out according to your own unique view and perspective.

Remember, you are a writer, or would like to be a writer. You have unlimited potential.

You are a super-hero, and you have the power to influence the thoughts, and to some extent the actions, of other people. On top of that, there has never been a better time in history to be a writer. You can publish your book electronically on several different platforms at zero cost. In the past, just getting your book printed meant spending a lot of time and some significant money sending manuscripts to publishers, or spending enough money to get 500 to 1000 copies printed for a first printing, with no guarantees of even a single sale.

If you want to see your book in print, you can use a Print-On-Demand (POD) publisher, such as CreateSpace, that will print your books one at a time as orders come in. This is truly an amazing time to be a writer.

I have studied the topic of successful writing models for a number of years. The following should help you discover the best models and incorporate them into your writing and the bookshelf that you will be writing yourself.

The Seven Habits

Start with the end in mind! That is the first of seven habits discussed by Stephan Covey in his International Bestseller, *7 Habits of Highly Successful People*.

You want to be able to sell your book when it is done. There are principles that will make writing a book that sells much easier and more likely.

1. Select a topic that is popular.
2. Select a niche in that topic that has a lot of interest.
3. Model the titles, covers, and descriptions of your books after other successful books.

Those three principles will keep you on track with producing a book that will sell.

The Book Thief

How to Steal the best ideas for books

You have heard the expression, "don't re-invent the wheel", haven't you? How long would it take to really create new vehicles if you had to come up with brand new ways of making them roll? The truth is, you need the foundations that have been laid for you by others that have come before. If you expect to do more and to get further, you have to leverage the work of others.

"If I have seen further than others, it is by standing on the shoulders of giants." -- Sir Isaac Newton.

When I was in Mexico City, I discovered the Zócalo. It is the city center where the national palace stands, and where they have excavated some old ruins. Mexico City was founded on top of the Aztec Empire. It has beautifully enhanced what was there originally and made it something much more and greater, but make no mistake, it is built on the foundation that the Aztecs created for it — down to some of the original water ways.

Insurgent

Steal the best models. They are successful for a reason. You have lots of room for unimaginable uniqueness, but let it fit within the framework that people are expecting. Let the format, how and where to find the information be familiar, while letting the content and perspective be what differentiates your work.

For non-fiction the following formats or models work very well:

The Problem-Solution book

A very successful model is the problem-solution model. So many people have problems and they are looking for good solutions. I list this one first because it is one of the most successful models and is often used for nonfiction books.

Why a Problem—Solution Book?

The recommendation from many authors is to write about one problem and present one solution. The reason is focus. If you present one problem and the solution to that problem, and keep that the focus of your book, you will be able to connect with the readers that are really interested in solving that problem. You will be able to describe that one problem, and present one solution. Your readers will not get lost, they will get what you promise in your book description.

People often have painful and annoying problems. You can be the solution to those problems and a key motivator to seeing them do something about the problem. It is important that you try to be very specific in these kinds of books. If you have specific steps to solve the problem, present those steps one by one so that the entire process can be followed precisely by your reader. Because one problem — one solution books with easy to follow steps are so popular, I wrote an entire book about how to quickly and easily write them. You can see that book here on Amazon:
http://www.amazon.com/dp/B00I0MKFVY .

There really are books about solutions for almost any topic. You can find them on the Internet at the Amazon.com marketplace. I'm going to have you spend some time on the Amazon.com site so that you can see a number of models that you can follow.

There is a trick that I want to share. When you open up the Amazon search page at Amazon.com, select Kindle store in the dropdown list next to the search bar. Then type in any topic that you are interested in, then select a link that looks like little thumb-nail boxes, then click Go.

Here is a screen shot so that you can see what I am talking about.

Figure 10 Amazon Settings

When the results show up, you will see a page of results, maybe 50 to 100 at a time.

I find this view useful when I am doing research. I can use it to pull up topics of interest and begin to see patterns and similarities between books as I scan them. Go ahead and try it once just to get the feel of it.

The Book of Tips and Tricks

A quick and simple type of book to write is a book of tips and tricks. This type of book can be written quickly because you won't need to go into a lot of detail. It can be very useful to readers because it delivers a number of related items that the reader may not have thought of in the past, or may not have associated with the particular topic.

I like to take pictures, and enjoy magazine articles and helpful books that explain how to catch the light the right way on my subjects, which perspectives to use and how to frame subjects with their surroundings. The little helps and hints usually make my pictures better, and help me improve my photos.

I'm also like a lot of other people, I would like to trim a few pounds, but I hate dieting and don't get the exercise that I really should get. I appreciate books that help me select foods and ways of preparing foods that are more natural, that are less processed, and that are better nutritionally for me, so that I don't have to resort to "dieting."

I bring up these examples, because they are among the books of tips and tricks that I have read in the past. When I encounter new methods, new tactics, new strategies, or new applications of things I try to write them down. I keep files and/or notebooks filled with short notes about subjects that I am interested in. The notes remind me of the little tricks and tips that I have learned along the way, but also serve as a basis for books that I would like to write. They are the tidbits that often help me organize and flesh out nonfiction books, but they can form a book all on their own.

There really are a lot of hints, tips, or tricks books out there for almost any subject imaginable.

Here is an Amazon Search that will bring up a number of books full of tips on a number of subjects:

http://www.amazon.com/gp/search/ref=sr_il_ti_
digital-
text?rh=n%3A133140011%2Ck%3Atips&keywo
rds=tips&ie=UTF8&qid=1395972721&lo=digita
l-text

The Book of Question and Answers

Do you know your ideal customer? It is worth taking some time to discover who that ideal customer is. Here is a way to kind of zero in on your ideal customer. Your ideal customer will depend on the topic you want to write about.

Type the name of that topic into the Google search bar, then type in the word blog. For example, if your topic was flower arranging, you would type "flower arranging blogs" in the Google Search field. You should get a list of blogs dealing with that subject in the search results.

Now go to Alexa.com and enter the names of the blogs in the Alexa search field. You should get back information about the number of visitors to each blog and some demographic information about those visitors.

Here are the types of demographic information that you can get from Alexa.com:

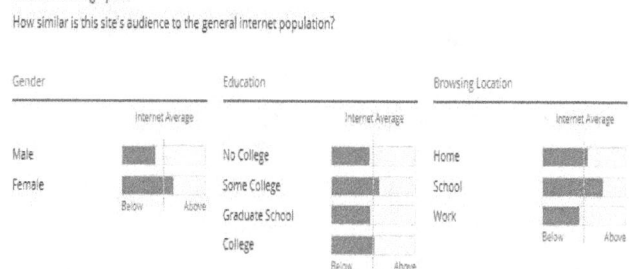

Figure 11 Alexa Demographics

With this information, you can begin to form a picture of your ideal customer. The most common visitors to these blogs will be your ideal customer. You might repeat this exercise with five or six of the blogs to see if the information co-ordinates. I like to imagine my ideal customer before writing my book. I even like to think of someone that fits those very characteristics, so that when I am writing, I can write as if I were talking to that particular friend.

Why is knowing your ideal customer important? Because now you can dig into what really bothers them. You can search on Yahoo Answers, on Forums, and on the blogs that you just listed.

Look for the things that really frustrate and annoy them. What questions do they raise continually? What scares them and keeps them up at night?

Gather your list of questions from every source available. Here you need to use the creativity method introduced earlier in the book of asking the right questions. Are there any other questions that these questions lead to? Using your ideal customer as a filter, prioritize your questions. Now you have an easy way to make a question and answer book.

Focus on the most pressing questions first, that will draw your readers in. Look at their motivation, why do these people need this information? Why are these questions so perplexing? Are there multiple answers? Are there reasons that some answers will be right for a certain group of these people, while other answers will be better for a different group? What group does your ideal customer fall into?

Again, go to Amazon.com and look at other books on the subject. What questions are they leaving out? Can you answer the same questions with an answer that would better fit your ideal customer?

The question-answer type of book has been around for a long time. Go out to Amazon and search on a topic of interest to you and append the word "question" (without the quotation marks) on to the end of the search term. You should see multiple question-answer books in the search results.

The Instruction Manual

I have bought and read many how-to books, and read many instruction manuals. I use them regularly to improve my skills in writing, marketing, and in a lot of everyday things like gardening and keeping up my cars.

Most people have a list of things they would like to know how to do. A how-to book is a set of instructions that break down big tasks into easy to perform instructions.

Here is a section of the table of contents for the book APE – Author, Publisher, Entrepreneur.

6. How to Write Your Book

7. How to Finance Your Book

8. How to Edit Your Book

9. How to Avoid the Self-Published Look

10. How to Get an Effective Book Cover

11. Understanding Book Distribution

12. How to Sell Your Ebook Through Amazon, Apple, Barnes & Noble, Google, and Kobo

13. How to Convert Your File

14. How to Sell Ebooks Directly to Readers

15. How to Use Author-Services Companies

16. How to Use Print-on-Demand Companies

17. How to Upload Your Book

18. How to Price Your Book

19. How to Create Audio and Foreign Language Versions of Your Book

Figure 12 How-to Table of Contents

See how most chapters start with a How-to sentence. This is what a how-to book might look like with every chapter dedicated to how to do some aspect of the overall theme of the book.

What makes this model so easy to follow, and often so usable by readers, is that it is usually pretty easy to break down any big process into a lot of small processes, and teach people how to do each of those smaller things that make up the whole.

Readers will often like this type of treatment. Why? Because they can skim over the things that they might already know, or aren't as curious about and get right to the meat, or the part of the book that they really wanted to read.

Most of us are over-busy. It seems that we all have full plates—but everyone also needs information.

Books are a great source of information, and even better if they are so well organized that a reader can know by browsing the table of contents that what they really need to find out is actually covered in the book. Notice in the example above, that each chapter is very specific. What you are going to learn from each chapter is spelled out exactly.

I know a lot of people like to make their chapter headings creative and mysterious. That may be a great idea for a fiction book, and might be OK for a number of types of nonfiction books, but when you are writing a how-to book—keep it simple and to the point.

Set the expectations with the chapter headings and provide great, actionable content so that your users feel that you really delivered.

The Benefit Promise Book

"The man or woman with sight see things as they are. The man or woman with insight see things as they could be."
     --Joseph P Martino

What would it take to see yourself 20 pounds lighter? What would it take to see yourself more confident? What would it take to see yourself debt-free? The book that catches your eye, usually has a hint of the promise of seeing yourself in a better situation after you read the book.

A book's title, the cover, and the book description have to make a promise to the reader. The promise can be spelled out and blatant, or it can be implied — regardless, it has to make a promise, then deliver on that promise.

Take a moment and browse Amazon's nonfiction books. You can get there by opening a browser to Amazon.com. Then select Kindle Store from the drop down. Next select Kindle eBooks, then best sellers, then nonfiction. The screen will look like this:

Figure 13 Amazon Nonfiction Screen

Browse through the nonfiction best sellers. Which ones jump out at you? What is the promise they make through the title and the cover?

Simple titles that overtly convey the benefits of the book might look like this:

Overcome Over-Eating, Lose 20 pounds In Two Weeks, Have More Confidence Around People, Or Find Peace Through Meditation. The benefit is clearly pronounced in each of these titles. One of them states a time period over which a reader would receive the benefit, if they apply the principles taught.

Write down the titles of the books that pique your interest. Write underneath the titles the promises being made either directly or indirectly. This will help you get used to the methods used by the titles and the covers that are successful today.

Dynasty

For fiction there are a number of genre. Fantasy/Adventure, Mystery, Drama, Romance, Science Fiction, Western, Historic, and many more. Wikipedia has a much bigger list: http://en.wikipedia.org/wiki/List_of_literary_g enres. Each genre has important aspects that readers of that genre expect. There are also some mixtures of genre, Sean Platt and Jonny Truant created their Unicorn Western, where they mixed Fantasy and Western. They seem to have a readership that continues to follow them through the continuing course of their series.

In fiction, it is important to know and understand the audience that you are writing for. J.K. Rowling targeted the Young Adult audience. Due to her success, many authors have followed her lead.

Once established, stay true to your audience. It is much easier to sell another book to someone who likes your writing, and is very interested in buying the next thing that you put out, than to find new readers to try your writing for the first time.

The Goblet of Fire

How to Pick Hot Topics and Niches

If you want to sell your eBooks, then you will have to write them in niches and about topics that are popular. Where are the best places to find those popular niches? Here are a few ideas:

Bestsellers

Amazon is proud of the books that are selling well. They have a list of the top 100 bestsellers AND the top 100 bestsellers in every category (and the number of categories keeps growing).

Amazon's best sellers can be found at http://www.amazon.com/best-sellers-books-Amazon/zgbs/books .

Keywords

Type a keyword into the Amazon search tool. After setting the category to books or Kindle Store, type in your subject or theme. The top books that come up are usually the most popular books associated with those keywords.

Click on the first book in the search results. Look down the listing to the best seller rank. Is the best seller rank below 50,000 for the top books from that keyword? Is it below 20,000? If there are a number of books with a best seller rank of less than 50,000 in the list of books returned from that search, then the keyword that you searched on is probably a decent keyword.

If there are a few books in the top 20 book titles returned that are below the 20,000 best seller rank mark, then that is probably a hot keyword.

Although the best seller rank is not a perfect metric for understanding how well the book is selling, and because the volumes of books sold fluctuate on a daily basis, there is no chart that will match up this metric to how many books are sold each day.

Here is a chart reproduced from Theresa Ragan. It is similar to other charts that I have seen, but keep in mind it is only a rough estimate. You can see the chart here:

http://www.theresaragan.com/2013/06/sales-ranking-chart.html .

The numbers below are based on indie authors who have been willing to share their numbers.

Amazon Best Seller Rank 50,000 to 100,000 - selling close to 1 book a day.
Amazon Best Seller Rank 10,000 to 50,000 - selling 3 to 15 books a day.
Amazon Best Seller Rank 5,500 to 10,000 - selling 15 to 30 books a day.
Amazon Best Seller Rank 3,000 to 5,500 - selling 30 to 50 books a day.
Amazon Best Seller Rank 500 to 3,000 - selling 50 to 200 books a day.
Amazon Best Seller Rank 350 to 500 - selling 200 to 300 books a day.
Amazon Best Seller Rank 100 to 350 - selling 300 to 500 books a day.
Amazon Best Seller Rank 35 to 100 - selling 500 to 1,000 books a day.
Amazon Best Seller Rank 10 to 35 - selling 1,000 to 2,000 books a day.
Amazon Best Seller Rank of 5 to 10 - selling 2,000 to 4,000 books a day.
Amazon Best Seller Rank of 1 to 5 - selling 4,000+ books a day.

Amazon Search Hints

When you go to the search bar in Amazon and start typing in the search field, Amazon begins to give you hints. A drop down list of up to 10 items begins to appear. The ones near the top have the most search volume that is why Amazon suggests them first.

Write down the ones that stick out to you, or write down the entire list. You can dig in a little deeper by typing your keyword, space, then the letter a. All of the suggestions for keyword + a will appear below the search bar. Now do it again for keyword + b. Continue through the alphabet.

Use the keywords that you find in your title, subtitle, description, and table of contents. You want Amazon to show your book to would be buyers often. If those sections of your book correspond to the words that people search for on Amazon, you will have a better chance of people seeing your book.

Categories

When you put your book up on Amazon, you will pick two categories that it can go under. You have to be able to categorize it according to what it is about, but there is plenty of latitude to find the most popular categories. There is a balancing act here.

You want to put your book in a category where it will show up in the top results, but the category has to be popular as well. It is no use being the top book in a category, if the entire category sells only 10 books per month. But, much worse than that, is being in a category where your book doesn't even show up in the top 100 or top 1000.

Best seller lists

Every category has a best seller list. Being in the best seller list can really pop sales, especially being the #1 best seller in the category. When you are the #1 best seller in a category, you get a little banner that Amazon displays with your book. It looks like the one below:

Write a Step-By-Step Book: Write Fast, Write Better, Write More, Solve Problems, Write Bestsellers, Learn How... by Dean R Giles (Jan 20, 2014)

Figure 12 Best Seller Banner

How to pick hot topics or niches

If writing a book that sells well depends on finding niches or topics that are hot or trending, then you are going to need to spend a little time finding those topics.

Hunger Games

Mark Joyner, in *The Great Formula,* said to first find a thirsty crowd, then sell them a glass of water. That is truly the secret formula. Find people that are hungry for what you have, and help them find it.

The internet is the place that people who buy eBooks are hanging out. You have got to find the hangouts of the people who are your ideal customers. Those hangouts are web pages, blogs, forums, authority sites, social media, and etc.

To find the webpages that are important to your niche or topic, it is as simple as pulling up a browser and typing in a keyword or phrase that has something to do with your topic. Google or Bing will try to find the most relevant pages on the internet about your topic.

These will usually be the pages with the most traffic for your topic as well, however, once you go to a page that is relevant in the search engines for your topic or keyword, you will want to follow up with that site by typing in the URL of the site into Alexa.com. Alexa will give you an estimate of the number of visitors to the site.

Sharpen the Saw

How to Develop an Author Mind Set

Do you see yourself as an author? Do you see yourself with multiple books to your name? If you can't believe it, why should anyone else? You have to start the process by believing in yourself. Even if you have to start with only a desire to believe, plant that desire deep within your heart. You want to write a book. You can write a book and publish the book.

You can do it. There is a book within you straining to get out—you have the power and the capacity to bring that to pass.
It will take some work, some organization, some discipline, some writing, and some re-writing. Getting that book out will be a process, but it has to start somewhere. Let it start today. Let it start here.

Apply the creativity principle of self-affirmation. Modify the exercise found in the chapter entitled "Assertions and Affirmations" with one change. Instead of writing that you are a creative person, you will write that you are a great writer. Be sure to use first, second, and third person sentences. Write it twenty different ways, and write it twenty different ways every day for three weeks. If you ever start to doubt your capacity as a writer, come back to this exercise.

Creating a Habit of Writing

"You are what you repeatedly do." this quote by Aristotle is something that I try to live by. There is a second one that helps me along as well. "That which we persist in doing becomes easier to do, not that the nature of the thing has changed but that our power to do has increased."

> --Ralph Waldo Emerson

Write Every Day

You have the same 24 hours per day that everyone else has. Of course you are busy, so is everyone else. Do yourself a favor, and set aside a time and write during that time every day. That will begin to create your daily habit. In fact, write it on your calendar or day planner. Get it in writing. This is the time that you are going to work on your writing.

Let your family know. Let others know. Don't compromise your writing time to any other activity.

Create the Environment

Turn off your cell phone, turn on your computer and shut down your browser. Turn off email alerts. Shut your door, shut out the distractions. You are now in the zone, and the more you practice getting into the zone quickly so that you can write, the faster you will be able to do it.

One of the things that helps me the most, is that the last thing I do before I close up and stop writing is to take a few minutes to outline what I want to cover next when I pull up my word document to start typing the next time. When I know where I'm going and what I plan to do the very next time I start writing, there is none of the classic overhead time of coming back and trying to remember where I left off.

I actually try to write in 15 to 30 minute intervals. I try to focus on just getting it down on the paper (in the Word document) for a straight 15 to 30 minutes — then I take a five minute break. I feel like I earned the break, and I feel refreshed when I get back to writing. This works for some authors, but not all authors.

When I read it the first time I thought to myself, "that would just kill my focus. I just barely get started in that 15 to 30 minutes." But, what I found was actually happening is that I was sitting and staring at a blank screen for those 15 to 30 minutes, just mulling over what I was going to say. Changing my paradigm so that I sit down and immediately start to write has made a big difference.

Now, I am able to start right up, and that little bit of time that used to be wasted is now actually productive time that gets the most work done. I also know that I will get a break soon -- so it is important to start writing right away.

Even when I'm not sure exactly what I want to say or how to say it, I start with what is in my head. As I start to write, it becomes clearer. In those times when what goes down on the paper isn't as clear as it should be, I find that I can fix it later, when I get to the editing part.

Create a Collection Swipe File

I study copywriting. I have been a lousy implementer of it, but one of the things that I have learned that has been the most use to me has been the concept that is called a swipe file in copywriting terms.

It actually means a file filled with headlines that can be "stolen" and modified to fit any situation.

The files that I keep, I call collections. I simply study, read, and pay attention to the things that I love and enjoy. When something strikes me or interests me, I write it down in my files. I try to keep files on the topics and subjects that I want to write about, but some of my files are more general.

In them I keep quotes, ideas for books, stories, poems, and words of wisdom. I draw from these files as I write my books. I have more than just files, I have journals, notebooks, 3X5 cards, sticky notes, and various other media on many devices. When I write, I will pull out my files, my cards, my notes, and put them around me. They are there for my support, and help me find the components, stories, examples, and other things that I will add to my writing.

How to Take Notes

Keep a notebook with you. When you run into a good idea, a phrase, or something that you like, write it down. It may not be of any use to you today, but it could help you a lot in the days ahead.

Keep a journal. Re-reading my journal helps me remember how I felt on my creative days, and helps me re-live those memories that I want to portray in books.

Write things on note cards. I feel that the digital world sometimes steals from the physical experiences that we can have. I love the feel of paper, newspaper, magazines, and real books. I copy bits and pieces of what I read onto note cards. Note cards are easier to sort, and I can spread them around and see what I am working with as it is laid out around me.

When you are taking notes, write down what you feel or what comes to mind, don't censure your writing at this point, just put it down. As you meld those thoughts into your work, just let it flow. Don't start to edit on the first draft— simply get it down.

I call this the SPLAT method. Get the ideas and thoughts splatted down into your document. Keep compiling as it comes to mind and as it feels like it is flowing. There will be time for editing, rearranging, and getting everything into its proper order. Don't do that when you are taking notes, nor in the very first draft.

Read and Study What You Love

How to write a book that everyone loves

Stephen King, in his book *On Writing* mentioned that the key was to read, read, read. What he meant was that it is infinitely easier to write if you read a lot. Reading will make you a better writer and will introduce you to other people's ideas.

What genres do you read now? Try to expand your reading, and try a different genre. Also dig deeper into what you do love. Read about your favorite author. When he mentions a book that was instrumental in forming his ideas, read that book. Look in the back of your favorite books, and follow the bibliographies. Read some of those books.

You will begin to become more knowledgeable in the topics you are interested in, and you may begin to see where the people that you admire got their ideas.

There are things that you love. Study those things. Copy and imitate them. As you try to imitate them you will discover what is uniquely you and yours along the way.

Twilight

How to Develop the "Dawning" of Your Next Book

Nonfiction Bestseller TOCs

What if you had a blue print that could map out the structure of a very successful book? What could you do with that kind of a blue print? The truth is every book has that kind of a blue print. It is called a table of contents. The table of contents is both a synopsis of the book and it is also a map of the book's organization.

Find the best books in your genre, on your topic, or about a theme that you are interested in. You can find those books on the Amazon.com site, at the library, and at book stores. Thanks to the Amazon "Look Inside" feature, you can find the table of contents to each of those books. You can also find tables of contents in those books at the library.

I always have a few books checked out. The library is one of my favorite places to hang out. You can also find the table of contents in those books at book stores.

I try to copy two to three tables of contents every day. If I can collect six to ten on the same subject or topic I will print them out. Then I will cut each entry out. I will re-arrange all of the entries on the table. I will group the ones that go together, or seem to be very much alike. I will begin to build my own structure using these sentences as my basis.

Once I have a good organization, I will create a hierarchy of ideas and concepts. I will use the SCAMPER creativity method found earlier in this book. I use this method to create completely unique sentences for my "Table of Content" or my book map.

Even one step further, I will look for a second topic to force fuse into my main topic to better target a specific audience or to make my work that much more unique.

Even if you never really use any of the ideas in the tables of contents that you copy out — you will, through daily association, get an intuitive feel for what a good table of contents should be like.

You will learn through each copy, and find yourself and your own style at the end of the copy.

Rewrite chapter headings, making them better

Once you have a good organization. Start improving your map. How can you make each chapter or chapter heading more enticing, more explicit, and more irresistible? Draw your readers in with each heading and sub-heading.

Read Every Day

If writing every day is an important habit, then reading every day is even more important. You can't draw from a vacuum. You need to feed your brain. If you do, it will take good care of you.

While you are reading save your favorite quotes, put down ideas as they come to you.
Keep a reading journal, and fill it up day after day. You will be surprised at how a reading journal will help you form new ideas and articulate those ideas until they are ready to be put into a book and published.

Remember to read what you love. Find the authors that entertain and enlighten you, that speak to your interests. Then study what makes each of them tick. You will discover more about yourself as you dig into the lives of those that influenced your thinking or the thinking of the world in the past.

Sea of Monsters

How to Make Your Book Get Noticed

Remember that your book has to stand out. It needs an outstanding cover, an amazing title, and a great description. You have probably heard of the 80/20 rule. The rule states that 80 percent of the results comes from 20 percent of the work. In the case of the three attributes mentioned above, that saying holds true.

When someone searches for your book online, the cover and the title have less than a fraction of a second to entice people to read the description. The description has about two to three seconds to convince people to click on the look inside feature. The look inside feature has four to six seconds to sell the book.

The crux of this process is in the cover and the title.

The Cover Story

How to create a killer cover

A little research here can go a long way. Select the books category in the Amazon search bar, then type in the topic you are interested in into the Amazon search bar. Click on the small box icons so that you get the display of thumbnail pictures across the screen.

Using the creative technique "slice and dice," introduced earlier in the book, break the cover down into its component attributes.

Here is the list of attributes that I use:

Colors
Images
Style
Text
Message (explicit or implied)
Layout
Elements

Colors: What are the dominant colors in the covers of the top 20 books on your topic? If some colors show up more than others, write down the colors, and try to mimic those colors in your cover.

Images: If your book is on dieting, you might see images of fruits and vegetables show up often. Maybe tape measures or scales to suggest losing weight or losing inches. Perhaps you will see images of people with near perfect bodies, or men touting defined ab muscles. Take note of the images that are the most popular. Maybe even jot down how many times those images appear in the top 20 to 30 books about your topic.

Style: Is the style of the most popular book covers full of energy or conservative? Are they edgy and suggestive of change or modernism? Are the covers generally more serene? Do they suggest happiness and a successful outcome? Are the images and feeling of the cover modern, futuristic, or looking back at a simpler past?

Text: Is the text loud? Does it take up most of the real estate on the cover? Is the text the most important part of the cover, or is it just a sideline to the images?

Message: Does the cover convey a message? If you read this will you be successful? Does the cover show what you might end up with if you apply what is in the book? Do the covers generally have a common theme?

Layout: Is the image central or the text? Do the covers have similar elements in them? Do they each have multiple images or just one central image? Do multiple covers have similarities in over all look?

Elements: What elements are present? Are there horizontal or vertical bars? Headers, footers, raised text, metallic colors? Are there any elements that seem to be repeated often?

You want your cover to have some similarities with the ones you have been looking at. You want your cover to look like it fits in—but you want some elements that make it stick out. Consider what you could emphasize that would tell your story better, and better express immediately the major benefits of your book.

The cover, the title, and the subtitle are the three things that you can use to influence someone to look a little closer at your book, and you have about two seconds to do that influencing. I would suggest getting a cover done professionally.

There are a number of professionals on Odesk.com, and Elance.com. I have actually had some very good covers created by people on Fiverr for five dollars. I have had the best success when sorting the gigs by number of reviews (lots of reviews is much better than few to no reviews).

I have also learned to be very explicit. Mention each of the attributes listed above, then include a screen-shot of the covers that could serve as a model for what you want.

Revenge

How to Modify Popular Book Titles in Your Niche

The popular titles are popular for a reason. Here is a great place to apply the creativity SCAMPER methods. Remember that stands for Substitute, Combine, Adapt, Modify, Minimize, Put to other uses, Eliminate, Revise and Reverse.

Substitute

Can you rewrite the popular title with different words? Break the title down into individual words, then break out the thesaurus. Can you find substitute words that have about the same meaning? Can you substitute other popular phrases that can mean something similar, but have even more meaning to a more modern crowd?

Combine

Combining ideas and elements from two popular titles can create a new popular title. The idea of combining two separate ideas to create a new one is called "force-fuse" by Keith Sawyer. The concept works very well for books.

Look for remote connections between two different subjects. Can the two be connected at the intersection of that remote connection?

Open your Amazon Search Page. Select the books or Kindle search type. Type in the name of your topic or keyword. Put the search page into the thumbnail view so that you have dozens of books and titles displayed. Write down the top 20 titles that actually have something to do with your topic.

Can you combine two or more titles in their current form? You will have to change things after you have combined the titles so that you aren't using the exact name of someone else's book encapsulated in your title, but it could suggest a title that would encompass both ideas.

Another way to look at it is to break the titles into smaller pieces. Now can you connect two or more pieces to create a good title, or great idea for a title? Finally, break the titles into individual words. Now can you combine words to make a good title that is completely unique?

Adapt

What are the popular titles leaving out? Could you adapt a title to include one more important concept? What do the current popular titles suggest? Can you adapt one or more titles to express that suggestion more concretely. Can you adapt a title to a specific popular group or interest? Do you see any gaps that are not being filled? For example, perhaps you see a beginner's book on a subject, and an advanced book about the same subject. Could this be a good place for an intermediate book? What audiences aren't being served? How can you serve that audience?

Modify

Can you modify one or more of the popular titles to focus more on an aspect that you want to write about? Can you modify a title to better express the key benefits of the book? Can you modify a popular title to make it more exciting, more enticing, more attention grabbing? What else could you modify about the popular titles that would make them more concrete, and/or better suited to a specific audience?

Minimize

What can you reduce from the popular titles? Can you reduce the number of words? Can you minimize any negative connotations in the current titles? Can you make any of the titles more concise? Can you make any of the current titles easier to understand?

Put to other uses

When writing your book you need to target a specific audience. Are you writing for adults with children, the single crowd, young adults, etc. The more specific you are about your audience the better you will be at writing directly for them. Once you have a successful title written for one of those audiences, look at a list of potential audiences, and ask: How could I change this to speak directly to a different audience. Steven and Sean Covey did a great job of that by following up the very successful *Seven Habits of Highly Successful People* book with a *Seven Habits of Highly Effective Teens*, then the *Seven Habits of Happy Children,* etc. The Chicken Soup for the Soul Series has books aimed at many different audiences with lots of tittles that begin with *Chicken Soup for the Soul*, targeting other audiences, or enticing many of the purchasers of the original book to purchase more books.

Another way to put information to other uses is to look for other industries that it can be applied to. Often information that applies to say, home building, could be modified to apply to home modification, decorating, or the do-it-yourself industry. Look for other places to apply your knowledge and expertise.

Eliminate

"Creativity is Subtraction" --Austin Kleon

What part of this information can be broken apart and modified to stand on its own? Perhaps you can get rid of portions that are uninteresting or that don't really apply to what you want to convey to your readers.

Eliminating discussions about context or setting the stage, getting rid of wordy explanations or unneeded examples, ditching speculation, unproved theory, or controversial aspects of your theme or topic can take your work from something good to something great.

Revise

Revise the popular theories. Let people know what is wrong with them and why they fail to produce the expected result.

Revise how most books address your topic. If most of them talk about your subject from top to bottom, revise how you talk about it, and do it from bottom to top, from results to beginning. Or start from the middle, explain the most important aspects of your theme, why nothing works if these elements are missing, then put them into the overall context.

Reverse

Reverse the popular assumptions about different topics. The Nobel Prize winner for his discovery and proof that light was built out of individual particles, reversed his thinking, and later won a second Nobel Prize for proving that light was a wave!

Work backwards. Find the end result that you want, then work from that point forward. Explain why working from the end result forward will produce the best results in the least amount of time and effort.

50 Shades of Crazy

How to solve most popular problems

There are popular personalities that address modern issues. The issues are often controversial, but if these issues are brought up by the "talking heads" of the day, they could be popular enough to write about.

The popular topics of the day stream across our computer screens on MSN or other news programs. They are talked about by Dr. Oz and Oprah. They are published in popular magazines. Make a trip to the magazine isle at the supermarket or the library. Collect ideas dealing with people's biggest pains and problems. Be relentlessly helpful in connecting people with solutions to their biggest problems.

Divergent

How to be controversial

When it comes to information, people and audiences list towards controversy. Why is that? Because when there are multiple, conflicting, and sometimes diametrically opposed solutions for the same problem, then the right solution for any one person is not immediately apparent. In other words, it is easier to talk to people about subjects where there could be lots of different solutions, and where some of those solutions won't work for everyone. This keeps the conversation going, and it brings the conversation up again and again.

Some of the bestselling novels of their time were the ones that addressed the most controversial subjects of the day. Gone with the wind was a huge success because it addressed not only the controversial subject of slavery, but of the many faces of the war that pit father against son, and neighbor against neighbor, and was the only battle fought on American soil.

Fix the Flaws

Find common flaws in most books in your topic. Look at the 1 and 2 star reviews for the most popular books on your topic. Are the criticisms in these reviews about some aspect that the author ignored? Are the complaints about the book founded? Could you add a section to your book that would address the shortcomings of this popular book? Or could you write an entire book based on what the other popular book has left out or not addressed?

Myth Busters

What does everyone get wrong? Are there popular myths in your area of expertise? Is there something that logically makes sense but actually makes the problem worse? Dispelling the myths and helping people understand why what they learned in the past is wrong is a great way to win readers and help people out.

What flies in the face of conventional wisdom? When you look at a problem from a different perspective, you often see why the "conventional wisdom" and the canned answers don't work for a specific group of people. Address your book specifically to this group of people.

Explain why what they keep being told isn't working for them, and give them a better solution.

Minute to Win It

How to write faster

Let's face it. The real scarce commodity comes down to time. There is no way to buy, create, or otherwise conjure up any more time than the given 24 hours in a day. Most any other resource can be purchased or acquired. You must guard your time vigorously.

Investing your time in organization can change the world that you live in. Block out time for reading, writing, idea generating, and organizing.

Now, what if you could increase the number of words that you produce in your books every day? You would be making better use of your time, and you would be producing more in a shorter amount of time.

2K to 10K

Successful writers produce 2K or more words per day for their books.

What if you could increase that number to say 10K? Could that help you produce more?

The key to more productivity is simple organization. Often the hardest part is wondering what to write next and how to organize it. Put a little more time into the organization up front.

Create the Outline

Spend time creating your table of contents and mapping what you want to say into an outline. Work out the logical flow of where you want to go. You don't have to have any of the details, just the overall concepts. Are there concepts and principles that you have to discuss as a foundation? What has to come next? How will it all be concluded? When you have a great organization, you know what to write next. It is a proven fact that you can write faster when you know what you are writing, and how you are getting there, than when you have to stop or re-write because the organization isn't solid.

The Matrix

How to create your book physically before creating it digitally.

Break your creation into physical and digital. Start with a notebook, sticky notes, 3X5 cards, pictures, photos, and/or a large sheet of butcher paper. Start writing and connecting your ideas, and start organizing them. Let your hands do some of the thinking as you create some physical symbols, words, and pictures that get your ideas into "the big picture."

Think of the crime scene detectives who put everything on the "wall." This is the perfect way to see the big picture, to make connections and to begin to play with the organization.

When I do a good job at this stage, the creation feels a little bit like play, but the results are amazing. The over-all organization can be compiled and modelled. Sometimes the best organization isn't obvious.

Take a picture of your first organizational draft, then reorganize again. Take a picture on the second or third way you have the material organized. Once the material is well organized, writing the book is so much easier and faster. At this stage it is easy to remove duplicate material, because it is easy to see where to put it — if you just started with the writing, you would likely go in logical loops because of the breadth of what you want to say.

Shark Tank

How to involve others in the creative process of your book

Brain storming

Conventional wisdom states that two heads are better than one. It is usually the case that multiple people can come together to generate more ideas and eventually ideas that are more creative. Brain storming is a great way to generate those ideas and involve other people.

Get people together in a room. Ask them to come prepared to discuss a specific topic, theme, or problem. Set a time limit, and stick to the limit. Set boundaries.

Give people a framework—for example, let people know what your limitations are. If you are working on a mystery book, tell people the ideas have to relate to a certain time period and setting. List those things on a whiteboard that are your restraints.

When people start to participate and add comments, refrain from criticizing ideas. However, if the ideas are clearly outside of the restraints that were put on the board, just make the comment, do you really think that would fall within the stated restraint?

One of the advantages of brainstorming is that one idea leads to another. The time limit keeps people in the production mode, where they will continue to put out ideas quickly. Don't spend any time analyzing the ideas at this point. Never let a spirit of contention start in the group, quickly stop any criticism or back biting, and ask people to focus on putting out more ideas.

Ask the experts

Find experts in your field. You might find some online, on blogs or forums. You might find them in your home town, they might own a business or be a consultant. Pick up published books by the experts in your field. Search the forums and industry blogs to find the names of experts. Drawing on the expertise of others is very respected, and even encouraged, especially if you mention the name of the expert you are quoting or consulting with.

Second opinions

Get advice from more than one expert.
Sometimes the advice you get may be biased
because the expert has an agenda of his or her
own. Sometimes there are just plain multiple
answers to the burning questions that you want
to answer for your readers. Dig a little deeper
and ask "why", after you get the answers from
the experts. You may be surprised at what drove
that expert to the conclusion that they espouse.

Remove a resource

After brainstorming or discussing problems or
solutions, ask those participating to come up
with a new answer if one of the obviously
needed resources wasn't available to implement
the best alternative discussed during the
brainstorming session. This second step often
yields more creative ideas, because the
limitations will make people look beyond the
obvious.

The Hobbit

How to make the most of your drafts

The first draft is the hardest. Set specific times and schedules for working on your book. Block out that time every day, or every time you plan to do your writing. I find it best to work for at least 20 minutes at a time, then take a 5 minute break, unless the writing is flowing and then I continue until I feel that I need a break.

The few minutes between writing cycles helps me relax, and often helps me get ready for the next production cycle.

With the first draft, I usually do that behind closed doors, with no distractions and without sharing much about it with other people. I look for feedback, other sets of eyes, and additional ideas in draft number three or four.

I begin my editing after completing the first draft. The idea of the first draft is to get it all down into a document on the computer.

I call it the splat method. I take my organized table of content/outline, and start filling it in.

There will be places that I feel I need some research or some picture or something to insert into the document. I will put a place holder such as <picture> or <story> or <example> and that will let me know where the things that I need to research should go.

I like to write down my time, then see how many words I have added to the document. I keep a log that looks something like this:

Aug. 24, 2014, 6:45 am – 7:20 am – 420 words, 11:30am – 12: 40pm 894 words. Worked on SLAA
Aug. 26, 2014, 6:45 am – 7:30 am – 563 words. Worked on SLAA, copied TOCs for HN.
Aug 27, 2014 , 8:30 pm – 9:20 pm – 344 words. Worked on SLAA.

.

.

.

My goal is two writing sessions per day and 2000 words per day. I have had periods where I reach that goal daily, and others where I haven't even come that close. When I find those times that writing is hard or I'm not being very productive, I try to look at what is wrong.

Am I allowing too many distractions? Is this part of my book not as organized as it needs to be? Do I need to do a little more research to be able to talk confidently about the subject, or some sub-theme of what I am writing about? I try to remedy the problem, and watch for the results. If you aren't tracking your production, you won't realize what makes a difference when you make those changes in your routine.

Change up the environment

Other things that can help is changing up the environment. I will sometimes pack my laptop into the kitchen or out on the patio. I will take some time doing a little writing in a different environment.

Make some writing time adventurous by going to a neighborhood internet café, ordering some desert, and do some writing at the café. I like to take my lap top with me at lunch time. I will pack a lunch, find a quiet park, and just sit on the grass with my computer.

Send in the Clowns

How to make your book tons better by involving others in early access reading.

After your first draft is finished, and you have gone back and made all of the needed changes and insertions, it is time to get help from others.

I have seen authors put drafts on blogs where people can read them, mark them up, and leave comments. I have a list of beta readers that I send my drafts to. I always get a lot of good comments back. I reserve the right to make suggested changes, or to leave things the way that they are. The biggest key to leveraging this hidden source of great advice is to not be offended with the suggestions.

Yes, I get it. Your book is your baby, and it is extremely hard to hear anyone even suggest that your baby isn't perfect, but take it all with a grain of salt, and make the suggested changes when they seem right. I have had so much help re-wording and re-working my books, and I owe a big debt of gratitude to my beta readers.

The Karate Kid

How to polish your book for publishing.

The third and fourth drafts are where you tear the book apart looking for the run on sentences, the grammar mistakes, typos, and anything else that detracts from the flow of the book. I like to take some time off from looking at the manuscript after the second draft, so that I can look at it with fresh eyes for the third draft. I also find it helpful to read each chapter separately. I will often start with the last chapter, read it, then pick up the second to last chapter, read it, and so on up to the first. This also helps me see the book in a different light.

Finally, hire an editor. After everything that I can fix, and my early access readers catch, I like to hire a professional to finish the polish. Everyone expects near perfection in the book editing. This is an expense that will pay for itself.

Star Wars

How to send your work to galaxies far, far away

There are a number of places that you can publish your book. I suggest publishing on Amazon Kindle first, or at the same time that you publish on Create Space. The indie author scene is a great place to be and costs you nothing to get started. Amazon puts out a great free guide for publishing your book. You can download it here. http://www.amazon.com/Publish-Amazon-Kindle-Direct-Publishing-ebook/dp/B004LX069M/ .

Your book has to be in a certain format. The free kindle book listed above will teach you all about that format. I found it a little difficult to keep track of all of the minutia. I run all of my books through this inexpensive formatter. You can pick up your copy here. http://incomenow.org/KinstantFormatter .

However you decide to do it, just take the plunge and get your book published. That will be the best thing that you can do for yourself. It will boost your confidence as a writer, and will feel so good to say you are "Published."

Other digital places to publish are Barnes and Noble, Apple, Smashwords, and Kobo.

Get Your Book Printed

I absolutely love to see my books in hard copy. Create Space gives you a way to publish hard copy books, and will let you buy as many promotional copies as you want at a huge discount. There are other discount indie book publishers such as Lightning Source, but Create Space is easier, and free.

If you want your book in print, here is a link for Create Space, they will print your book on demand, so that it costs nothing to list, and you get a royalty with each sale.
https://www.createspace.com/ .

Traditional Publishers

What about going through a publisher and putting your book out the traditional way?

Traditional publishers still publish a lot of books. Their business is transforming, but what hasn't changed is that the vast majority of what they receive gets rejected. However, I have seen authors that get their start on Kindle, prove that they have potential, and then get picked up by a traditional publisher. You can consider finding an agent and trying to work with a big publisher.

The Book Shelf

How to keep your bookshelf growing

Every book that you produce becomes a new book on your personal book shelf. There isn't a feeling in the world that compares to looking over your own personal bookshelf and realizing what you have accomplished. Each book is an asset in your portfolio. It can make you money every day, but it is also an advocate to entice people to buy more of your books. The best way to be successful in the writing business is to write good books, then continue to put out more good books.

First of all, you become more experienced with every book that you write, and writing then becomes an everyday thing for you, it may even become an obsession.

Everything gets easier as you do it again and again. But most importantly, each new book teaches you new things, and helps you to understand more and more about just what kinds of books will be successful and what ones won't be as successful.

You begin to build your own writer's intuition. Each success leads to greater success and more enjoyment!

At the end of each of your books, ask for reviews, and put in links to your other books. If the reader likes your style and what you have done for them, it is very likely that they will want to read another of your books. Creating a following is an important part of being a successful author. Create the best product that you know how, then link those products together, helping your customers down that road that leads to the rest of the books in your bookshelf.

Sales by association

Visit a library or a book store. Do you notice that books that are similar are placed on shelves right next to each other. Where should your books be? What shelves would they be on? What books should surround them?

The Discovery Channels

How are you going to be found?

Honestly, among the hardest problems facing authors is the problem of being found. When you publish your book on Amazon it starts at the very bottom of the pile, #2,754,567 out of 2,754,567. Your book is in a hole on Amazon that no one will find on its own. Go out to the Amazon search page, and search for your book by subject. Which books came up on the first page of the search results? Are these books selling? Do they have an overall sales rank of 50,000 or less? If so, then you want your book to be associated with those books, provided they are actually about a similar subject.

Start with keywords in your title: Do an Amazon search with the main term or keyword for your theme. Now look at the results. Is the keyword in any of the titles that came up in the search results?

If it was in very few titles, you may want to consider that term or keyword in your title,

Amazon usually gives preference to a title with the exact word in it.

Think about the words that you would use to search on to find a book on your subject. Write down as many as come to mind. Does your description have any of those keywords in it? Does your table of contents contain any of those keywords? Look for ways to incorporate as many of those keywords as you can in the description and table of contents. Help Amazon know that your book belongs to that particular subject.

It is estimated that you have two to three seconds to capture someone's attention. Having the right keywords for the search will help, but having an amazing cover and a convincing title will make the most difference.

Ebooks on Amazon make it very easy to experiment with. Try a different cover. Try a different title. Keep track of when you changed the title or the cover. Record the number of sales, the number of free downloads, or times your book sold at a bargain after changing the title or cover. Which of the covers or titles did the best? Be sure to only change one thing at a time, and to give yourself a month or so after each change to have some good data to work with.

If your book were in the library or in the book store, it would be surrounded by other books like it. Choose a category that will associate your book with the books that you would like to see your book on the self with.

Many people would look at similar books as competition—look at them differently. Most people who buy one book on a subject, will end up buying many books on the same subject. You need to use that association, rather than resent it.

If you have a blog or guest write for a blog in that space, do a book review. Praise the similar book and its author in your review. Send the author a note on their blog, twitter, or Facebook account, letting them know that you wrote about their book, and send them a link to your article. If they like the article, they might link back to it. At the very end of your article, just casually mention to readers that if they liked this book, they are going to LOVE your book, or simply do what Amazon does. At the bottom of the article put a thumbnail image of your eBook cover, and say the people who bought this book (the book that your reviewed) also purchased this book (your book), and proudly display your eBook cover thumbnail and title with a clickable link back to Amazon where people can buy your book.

There is nothing better than to see your book as one of the five or so other books that Amazon shows their customers in the "people that purchased this also purchased… section. If you keep working at associating your book with other successful books in the space, you will begin to leverage their success, and your book will show up in that list on Amazon.

Born Free

How to Create Sales with Free Promotions

Welcome to the Kindle Direct Publishing (KDP) program. If you select the Kindle Direct Publishing you agree to only publish digitally on Amazon for 90 days. During those 90 days amazon will rent your book out and give you a portion of a pool of money designed for those rentals, it will put your book into the Kindle Unlimited Program where you get paid downloads there, and will give you 5 free promotional days.

With these 5 free promotional days, you can set up a free promotion. In the appendix there is a large list of sites that will list your free promotion, most of them are free. I find it takes a lot of time to list my promotion to each of those site, so I use one of the following $5 Gigs on Fiverr.com to have them post to the best 10 to 30 of those site.

https://www.fiverr.com/bknights/submit-your-free-kindle-book-to-the-15-best-kindle-promotion-sites?

https://www.fiverr.com/kindlepromoter/submit-your-kindle-book-to-30-top-kdp-promotion-websites

https://www.fiverr.com/koky1205/submit-your-free-kindle-book-to-20-best-kindle-promotion-sites

https://www.fiverr.com/timmybx/manually-submit-your-kdp-kindle-ebook-free-day-promo-to-15-kindle-book-sites

In the appendix I have listed a number of Facebook pages, groups, twitter IDs and hashtags that will sometimes get a few more eyes on your promotion. I will usually pay $5 for one of the following Gigs on Fiverr.com to do some social media for me on my promotion day.

I will use the Gig extras provided by bknights: https://www.fiverr.com/bknights/submit-your-free-kindle-book-to-the-15-best-kindle-promotion-sites?

Or one of these:

https://www.fiverr.com/melrock/promo-your-kindle-free-days-to-my-huge-social-network-twitter-fb-pin-and-blog

https://www.fiverr.com/bknights/promote-and-market-your-self-published-kindle-book-to-4800-active-kindle-readers-on-my-facebook-page-during-your-promo-or-marketing-period

https://www.fiverr.com/dziomek/promote-your-books-via-social-media

I usually use one or two of the promotional days per month over the 90 days. I find that the $5 to $15 investment pays back two to five times more sales than it costs. The real benefit being improved sales rank, after selling a few copies right after the promotion, which may sell more copies for the next few weeks. There are other paid promotions that I have done, some with great success, and others without recouping my initial investment, but your mileage will vary.

Places to advertise paid book promotions include:

Goodreads.com
BookBub.com
Ereader News Today
Kindle Nation Daily/Book Gorilla
BookBlast.com

A little promotion goes a long way. I like the $5 Fiverr.com Gigs because they are inexpensive and usually give me a return on my investment. Occasionally it is a really good return, with hundreds of downloads and dozens of sales. It was after one of these promotions that my *Write a Step-by-Step* book made it to #1 Best Seller in its category.

CONCLUSION

Steal the Best Ideas

Build on the ideas of others.
Steal their ideas.
Make them your own.
Then develop those ideas into something unique and better.

Use Principles of Creativity

Start from the inside.
Ask the right questions.
Use creativity tools.
See with a different perspective.
Learn deeply and broadly.
Create collections.
Follow your heroes.
SCAMPER

Apply Creativity to Writing

Use the best models.
Develop an author mind set and habits.
Leverage what you love.
Learn the best topics.

Modify what you find.
Create your book.
Publish your book.
Promote your book.
Grow your bookshelf.

You are an author, an innovator, and a super-hero. You shape the thoughts and can shape the actions of others with your words. Teach people correct principles, then encourage them to live those principles.

"The Secret: Do good work and share it with people." --Austin Kleon

Let your work speak for itself!

If you have enjoyed this book, please leave a review:

http://www.amazon.com/dp/B00NVN99FK

Reviews are so important to indie authors.

Thank you.
Dean

P.S.

Thank you for reading the entire book. I have a bonus gift for you!

Bonus Feature

Here is the first Chapter of "Write a Step-by-Step Book".

If you have enjoyed this book, you will love the first book in the series. Write a Step-by-Step Book. It is right to the point — if you want to write faster, be more effective, and create something that readers just love, you need to read Write a Step-by-Step book.

Here is the first chapter for reading enjoyment.

Write a Step-by-Step Book: Write Fast, Write More, Solve Problems, Write Bestsellers

By Dean Giles

Introduction

Break it down! Simplify! Spell it out! Make it easy to follow. If a picture is worth a thousand words, a model is worth a thousand dollars.

The world of nonfiction books is a world where people have difficult and vexing problems. They need real solutions to those problems, and they need someone that can show them how to solve those problems step-by-step.

I've read hundreds of nonfiction books. I have searched out the books looking for answers. I have found some of those books to be very entertaining, I have found others to be very informative, but the ones that have made my life easier and have changed my way of thinking were the ones with straight forward and simple instructions. These are the ones that sit on my bookshelf and that I return to again and again. They make great reference volumes, because they are, by design, compact and to the point.

Where most nonfiction books come up short is that they don't have specific enough instructions. They are usually really good at pointing out what the problems are and what benefits you, the reader, will receive when you solve your particular problems. But they are light on the specific, easy-to-follow steps that will actually solve the problem!

I also realized that, with those books, where the authors do a good job of presenting the problems and promise solutions, as a reader, I often get to a point where I am salivating—I have experienced that problem, I REALLY want the solution! However, by the end of the book, I am usually disappointed. It is true, that most books offer a solution, but rarely do they provide detailed enough instructions to really help me put the solution to work for me.

YES I KNOW: to solve my weight problems I simply have to eat fewer calories and increase exercise, to solve my money problems I simply must bring in more money and spend less, to solve my relationship problem I need to be kinder and think of others more often, to solve my career problem I need to show leadership and innovation, somehow all of that is so painfully obvious, and yet so mystifyingly illusive.

The truth is, each of us knows more than we realize. Each of us, for the most part, has a basic understanding of how things work. Sometime we DO need a better solution, but often, what we really need is a better way to implement what we already know. We need something that will entice us to work our way over the barriers, and actually put into action what we have learned.

That is where the step-by-step book comes in to play. Writing a step-by-step book solves a number of problems. For one thing, it simplifies the process for the author. For another, it makes the solution seem easier and more doable for the reader.
Step-by-step instructions seem more manageable. They can be accomplished one at a time. The reader can eat the proverbial elephant, one bite at a time, and avoid the inevitable "drinking from the fire hydrant" effect of the typical overload of information that comes from most informational books.

You Already Know Much of What You Will Need To Write – And It Is All Brilliant!

How many problems have you solved in your lifetime? Can you simplify the process of solving one specific problem to a set of steps that anyone could take to solve that problem? Can you add your own introduction to the problem by explaining what situations in your life led up to the crisis?

Were there some solutions that you tried that didn't work? Did others give you advice that helped you along the way, or did the advice not really help at all? How did you feel when everyone "had advice for you to solve your problem"? And how did it feel when you realized that for all the good intentions, the advice was obvious? What do you wish you had known before you started on the road to your ultimate solution? What were the results of implementing the solution? Can you summarize the steps and the results in a closing conclusion?

If you can answer the questions above, you can write a step-by-step book that will actually help a lot of people solve their biggest problems. If you suffered from a problem, then it stands to reason that lots of other people are also suffering from the same problem.

If you have solved that problem, you have a valuable solution that needs to be shared with others, and that others will gladly pay for!

Perhaps you might think that it would be embarrassing to write about a problem that you have experienced. That is a perfectly reasonable thing to feel. In that case simply write the book in the third person.
Explain that you helped a friend or an associate to solve this problem in their lives. Perhaps you could write your book as an accumulation of experiences from more than one person experiencing this problem.

You actually may be the go-to person that others come to when they experience these kinds of problems. In that way you become the local expert. You have information that others need. You can help others, and help yourself, by getting the solutions to these problems into an easy to follow step-by-step book.

And, what if you don't have all of the answers? That's OK too. I am going to show you the best places to quickly find the answers to those difficult problems, keeping in mind that the solutions are rarely new or earth-shaking. The best solutions are the simple, straight forward solutions, however, the magic comes in the presentation of the solution and how, exactly to implement the solution.

The magic really is in the step-by-step presentation that will motivate your reader to take those steps and make a change in his or her life. You can be that catalyst, and be the influencer that gets people to a better place through your book.

I am going to make one more bold statement. You actually need to publish your book as an eBook. Ebooks and Information Products are creating a new economy.

Amazon announced that they are selling more eBooks than physical books. People like John Locke and Amanda Hocking have self-published and sold millions of eBooks. Market places for eBooks can be found all over, from Clickbank, to Amazon, from JVZoo to Barnes and Noble, the opportunities for publishing and selling eBooks are almost endless, and the cost to publish an eBook can be absolutely nothing.

The biggest barriers to writing and publishing books have been removed with the no-cost eBook publishing. There are also some no-cost print-on-demand publishing solutions such as Createspace, to produce printed books.

There is really nothing stopping you from participating in and profiting from the new eBook economy and paradigm. I will show you, step-by-step how to write, publish, and ultimately profit from simple eBooks that are laser targeted to customers that will love your work, and perhaps buy everything that you write and produce.

Making the Mental Transition

There is a saying that everyone has a book inside them. When it comes to step-by-step books, it is much more likely that everyone has at least six books inside of them. How could that be, you ask? Think about the things that you are good at.

What do people come to you for help with? What hobbies do you have? What interests and passions? What associations are you a part of? What do you do for a living? What do you want to learn? It maybe that you can create your step-by-step eBook while you are learning something that you have wanted to learn for years.

I personally prefer books written by people who openly admitted that they started from square one (actually everyone does start from square one, you just don't hear about it), then they summarized what it took to find the information that they needed and what it took to become proficient at whatever they are teaching.

What stops most people from creating a book or a product is not knowing how to start and the simple fear of getting out of their comfort zone to do it.

In this eBook I am going to show you one step at a time how easy it is to create simple one problem-one solution, step-by-step, information eBooks that will really help other people, and will create a long-lasting income stream for you, the eBook creator.

Among the myths of eBook writing is the thought that an author must be an expert of some kind. This is false. A writer does have to have more knowledge than his ideal customer. If the customers weren't looking for additional knowledge than they already have, there would be no reason for the book. But a book can be interesting and informative if it contains just a few critical things: (End of Preview)

Read the rest here:
https://www.amazon.com/dp/B00I0MKFVY

If you have any feedback, questions, or just want to drop me a note, you can send an email to dean@austinsgift.com .

Other Books by This Author

About Writing

Write a Step by Step Book
https://www.amazon.com/dp/B00I0MKFVY
How to Steal Like an Author:
http://www.amazon.com/dp/B00NVN99FK
Discover Book Ideas:
http://www.amazon.com/dp/B00IODSNVI
Write On
http://www.amazon.com/dp/B00O9LIBMK

Not About Writing

Dragons Restored
http://www.amazon.com/dp/B014N2E9CU
Life's Poetry
http://www.amazon.com/dp/B00UU0UQ2C
The Snow Birthday
http://www.amazon.com/dp/B00BWAP6SS
Summer Time Fun
http://www.amazon.com/dp/B00DZVYG4W
Keyword Planner
http://www.amazon.com/dp/B00E45ADKE

Connect with me

Email: dean@autstinsgift.com
Blog: http://austinsgift.com
Facebook:
https://www.facebook.com/WriteAStepByStepBoo
k

Sign up for my email list:
http://AustinsGift.com

End Notes:

1
http://grammar.about.com/od/advicefromthepros/a/W
here-Do-Writers-Find-Their-Ideas.htm

Appendix

**** Note These Resources Change Constantly****

Places to Post Your Kindle Select Free Days

http://ereadernewstoday.com/ent-free-book-submissions/
http://www.fkbooksandtips.com/for-authors/free-kindle-book-submission-form/
http://digitalbooktoday.com/12-top-100-submit-your-free-book-to-be-included-on-this-list/
http://indiebookoftheday.com/authors/free-on-kindle-listing/
http://rastephensonauthor.blogspot.com/p/free-promotion-for-independent-authors.html
http://www.mybookandmycoffee.com/p/free-ebook-feature.html
http://freedigitalreads.com/author-submissions/
http://indieauthorbookreviews.wordpress.com/kindle-promo/
http://www.sevenbillionereaderbooks.com/free-kindle-book-submission/
http://www.pixelofink.com/sfkb/
http://bargainebookhunter.com/free-book-notification-form/
http://kindlenationdaily.com/kindle-nation-daily-free-and-bargain-book-listings/
http://www.freebooksifter.com/?c=7
http://www.dailyfreebooks.co.uk/promote-your-kindle-book.html

http://onehundredfreebooks.com/author-free-kindle-book-submission.html
http://www.ebookxp.net/submit.php
http://www.totallyfreestuff.com/submit.asp?m=0
http://www.icravefreebies.com/contact/
http://bargainebookhunter.com/feature-your-book/
http://addictedtoebooks.com/free#comment-3747
http://ebookshabit.com/for-authors/
http://www.theereadercafe.com/p/authors.html
http://www.freebookdude.com/p/list-your-free-book.html
http://www.frugal-freebies.com/p/submit-freebie.html

Facebook Pages to List Free Books On

These are quick and easy, just go to the pages on your free day, and put a link to your Kindle eBook in the post. They appear immediately.

https://www.facebook.com/Freebies4Mom
https://www.facebook.com/bookskindle
https://www.facebook.com/FreeBookFeed
https://www.facebook.com/KindleUtopia
https://www.facebook.com/pages/Free-Daily-eBooks/277545182364423
https://www.facebook.com/FreeEbooksDownloads
https://www.facebook.com/eReaderLove

https://www.facebook.com/KindleFreebies
https://www.facebook.com/ePublish.a.Book
https://www.facebook.com/pages/Free-Kindle-
Books-Updated-Daily/155923931093850
https://www.facebook.com/ourawesomegang

Places to Advertise Your Book

http://www.goodreads.com/
http://www.booktalk.com/authors/
http://www.kindleboards.com/
http://www.librarything.com/
http://www.authonomy.com/?from=bookarmy
http://www.booktalk.org/
http://www.booksie.com/
http://www.wattpad.com/
http://www.shelfari.com/
http://www.nothingbinding.com/
http://www.jacketflap.com/
http://www.whowrotewhat.net/
http://www.timgreatonforum.blogspot.ca/
http://www.writers.net/
http://www.bibliophil.org/
http://www.bookbrowse.com/
http://www.bookbuzzr.com/
http://www.filedby.com/
http://www.bookhitch.com/
http://savvybookwriters.wordpress.com/
http://www.bookreportradio.com/
http://www.timgreatonforum.blogspot.ca/
http://www.bowkerlink.com/
http://www.kindlemojo.com

http://blog.booksontheknob.org
http://addictedtoebooks.com/submission/
http://freebooksy.com/about/

Facebook Book Groups

https://www.facebook.com/groups/42628213743
2533/
https://www.facebook.com/groups/38934384778
2037/
https://www.facebook.com/groups/pageonepro
fits/
https://www.facebook.com/groups/BooksLuver
s/
https://www.facebook.com/groups/abrex/
https://www.facebook.com/groups/passionforb
ooks/
https://www.facebook.com/groups/childrenboo
kclub/
https://www.facebook.com/groups/Bookjunkie
sfreebies/
https://www.facebook.com/groups/bookplace/
https://www.facebook.com/groups/freetoday/
https://www.facebook.com/groups/27055833637
9692/
https://www.facebook.com/groups/15796058096
0255/
https://www.facebook.com/groups/memberswr
itersgroup/
https://www.facebook.com/groups/46959207307
4586/

https://www.facebook.com/groups/KidBooksWithGoodValues/

https://www.facebook.com/groups/AmazonBookClubs/

https://www.facebook.com/groups/187547284642012/

https://www.facebook.com/groups/booknest/

https://www.facebook.com/groups/174224899314282/

https://www.facebook.com/groups/623206594363552/

https://www.facebook.com/groups/ebooksrock/

https://www.facebook.com/groups/kindlemojo/

https://www.facebook.com/groups/2204546223/

https://www.facebook.com/groups/204725947524/

https://www.facebook.com/groups/booksgoneviral/

https://www.facebook.com/groups/iluvbooks/

https://www.facebook.com/groups/2204565182/

https://www.facebook.com/groups/320356974732142/

https://www.facebook.com/groups/179494068820033/

https://www.facebook.com/groups/bookjunkiepromotions/

https://www.facebook.com/groups/436402966439126/

https://www.facebook.com/groups/freebkrus/

https://www.facebook.com/groups/boomdom/

https://www.facebook.com/groups/370900356880/

https://www.facebook.com/groups/kindlemark
etingrevelations/
https://www.facebook.com/groups/ParaYourAb
normalAuthors/
https://www.facebook.com/groups/FreeTodayO
nAmazon/
https://www.facebook.com/groups/ReviewersR
oundup/
https://www.facebook.com/groups/9476163038/
https://www.facebook.com/groups/freeebooks/
https://www.facebook.com/groups/14021686533
33862/

Bibliography and More Resources

Giles, Dean, *Keyword Planner: How to Exploit Google Adwords Keyword Planner to Get Unlimited, Buyer-Targeted, Long-Tail Keywords,*
http://www.amazon.com/dp/B00E45ADKE/

Giles, Dean, *Write a Step-by-Step Book,*
http://www.amazon.com/dp/B00I0MKFVY/

Giles, Dean, *Discover Book Ideas,*
http://www.amazon.com/dp/B00IODSNVI/

Aaron, Rachel, *2,000 to 10,000: Writing Faster, Writing Better, Writing More of What You Love,*
http://www.amazon.com/2k-10k-Writing-Faster-Better-ebook/dp/B009NKXAWS/

Allen, Christopher David, *How to Publish a #1 Best Seller On Kindle – No Cost Publishing and Marketing Secrets of a Bestselling Author – How to Book and Guide for Smart Dummies,*
http://www.amazon.com/HOW-PUBLISH-BEST-SELLER-KINDLE-ebook/dp/B0089TESCU/

Beam, Mary Todd, *The Creative Edge: Exercises to Celebrate Your Creative Self*,
http://www.amazon.com/Creative-Edge-Exercises-Celebrate-Your/dp/1600611117/

Catmull, Ed, and Wallace, Amy, *Creativity Inc.: Overcoming the Unseen Forces that Stand in the Way of Creativity*,
http://www.amazon.com/Creativity-Inc-Overcoming-Unseen-Inspiration-ebook/dp/B00FUZQYBO/

Covey, Steven R., *7 Habits of Highly Effective People: Powerful Lessons in Personal Change*,
http://www.amazon.com/Habits-Highly-Effective-People-Anniversary-ebook/dp/B00GOZV3TM/

Csikszentmihalyi, Mihaly, Creativity: Flow and the Psychology of Discovery and Invention,
http://www.amazon.com/Creativity-Flow-Psychology-Discovery-Invention-ebook/dp/B000TG1X9C/

Eagle, Dennis and Villegas, Oliver, *7 Secret Steps to Best Selling Author*,
http://www.amazon.com/Secret-Steps-Bestselling-Author-Revealed-ebook/dp/B00EA1XGJW/

Epstein, Robert, *The Big Book of Creativity Games*, http://www.amazon.com/Big-Book-Creativity-Games-Jumpstarting-ebook/dp/B002KCFIB2/

Kindle Direct Publishing, *Building Your Book for Kindle*, http://www.amazon.com/Building-Your-Kindle-Direct-Publishing-ebook/dp/B007URVZJ6/

Kleon, Austin, *Steal Like an Artist: 10 Things No One Told You About Creativity*, http://www.amazon.com/Steal-Like-Artist-Things-Creative-ebook/dp/B0074QGGK6/

LJS Quote 2 Motivate, *Quotes For Writers: Inspiration, Advice, Humor, and Motivational Stories From Famous Authors*, http://www.amazon.com/Quotes-Writers-Inspiration-Motivational-Stories-ebook/dp/B00HFA4V9O/

Locke, John, *How I Sold 1 Million eBooks in 5 Months*, http://www.amazon.com/How-Sold-Million-eBooks-Months-ebook/dp/B0056BMK6K/

Michalko, Michael, *Thinkertoys: A Handbook of Creative-Thinking Techniques*, http://www.amazon.com/dp/1580087736/

Plat, Sean and Truant, Johnny B., *Write. Publish. Repeat.*, http://www.amazon.com/Publish-Repeat-No-Luck-Required-Self-Publishing-Success-ebook/dp/B00H26IFJS/

Hawker, Libbie, *Take Off Your Pants!: Outline Your Books for Faster, Better Writing: Revised Edition* https://www.amazon.com/Take-Off-Your-Pants-Outline-ebook/dp/B00UKC0GHA

Redwine, Kate, *Crush It With Kindle Publishing The Entrepreneur's Guide for Self Publishing Books on Kindle, and Promoting Your Book to #1 Bestseller Status*, http://www.amazon.com/Publishing-Entrepreneurs-Building-Promoting-Bestseller-ebook/dp/B00DH8STT6/

Rofe, Rachel, KInstant Formatter, http://incomenow.org/KinstantFormatter

Sawyer, Keith, *Zig Zag: The Surprising Path to Greater Creativity*, http://www.amazon.com/dp/B00BG62E9C/

Scott, Steve, *How to Discover Bestselling eBook Ideas – The Bulletproof Strategy*, http://www.amazon.com/dp/B009D6JL20/

Tardif, Cheryl Kaye, *How I Made $42,000 In One Month Selling My Kindle eBooks,*
http://www.amazon.com/Made-Month-Selling-Kindle-eBooks-ebook/dp/B0080USSYW/

Turner, Laina, *All I Know About eBook Marketing,*
http://www.amazon.com/All-Know-About-e-Book-Marketing-ebook/dp/B009VO9YGW/

Vulich, Nick, *Freeking Idiots Guide to Writing a Kindle Bestseller Tips and Tricks to Make Your Book a Bestseller in Its Category,*
http://www.amazon.com/Freaking-Writing-Bestseller-bestseller-category-ebook/dp/B00B1Z7YFM/

Williams, Glyn, *Bestseller Tactics: Advanced Self Publishing Techniques to Help You Sell More Books On Amazon and Make More Money. Advanced Author Marketing.*
http://www.amazon.com/Bestseller-Tactics-publishing-techniques-Marketing-ebook/dp/B00GHTL5O8/

Platt, Sean and Johnny B. Truant, *Fiction Unboxed: How Two Authors Wrote and Published a Novell in 30 Days From Scratch, in Front of the World*
https://www.amazon.com/Fiction-Unboxed-Publishing-Writing-Scratch-ebook/dp/B00OVHXEJW

Free eBooks That You Can Download

How to Write Book Descriptions:
http://austinsgift.com/book-descriptions

How to Publish a Kindle
http://austinsgift.com/how-to-publish-a-kindle

www.ingramcontent.com/pod-product-compliance
Lightning Source LLC
Chambersburg PA
CBHW071357280526
45787CB00001B/366